CliffsNo

Oedipus Trilogy

By Charles Higgins and Regina Higgins

IN THIS BOOK

- ■ Learn about the Life and Background of the Playwright
- ■ Preview an Introduction to the Plays
- ■ Explore themes, character development, and recurring images in the Critical Commentaries
- ■ Examine in-depth Character Analyses
- ■ Acquire an understanding of the Plays with Critical Essays
- ■ Reinforce what you learn with CliffsNotes Review
- ■ Find additional information to further your study in the CliffsNotes Resource Center and online at www.cliffsnotes.com

Houghton Mifflin Harcourt
Boston   New York

About the Authors

Charles and Regina Higgins have worked together as educational writers for 15 years. They both have Ph.D.s in English from Indiana Univeristy.

Publisher's Acknowledgments

Editorial

Project Editor: Linda Brandon
Acquisitions Editor: Greg Tubach
Copy Editor: Janet Withers
Editorial Administrator: Michelle Hacker
Glossary Editors: The editors and staff of Webster's New World Dictionaries

Composition

Indexer: York Production Services, Inc.
Proofreader: Janet Withers
Wiley Indianapolis Composition Services

CliffsNotes™ *Oedipus Trilogy*

Published by:
Houghton Mifflin Harcourt

www.hmhco.com

Copyright © 2000 Houghton Mifflin Harcourt

ISBN:978-0-7645-8581-4

Printed in the United States of America

DOC 20 19 18 19 17 16 15 14 13

4500476934

1O/TR/RQ/QW/IN

For information about permission to reproduce selections from this book, write to Permissions, Houghton Mifflin Harcourt Publishing Company, 215 Park Avenue South, New York, New York 10003.

Library of Congress Cataloging-in-Publication Data
Higgins, Charles.
    CliffsNotes Oedipus Trilogy / by Charles Higgins and Regina Higgins.
        p.   cm.
        ISBN 978-0-7645-8581-4 (alk. paper)
    1. Sophocles. Oedipus Rex--Examinations--Study guides. 2. Sophocles. Oedipus at Colonus--Examinations--Study guides. 3. Sophocles. Antigone--Examinations--Study guides. 4. Greek drama (Tragedy)--Examinations--Study guides. 5. Seven against Thebes (Greek mythology) in Literature. 6. Antigone. (Greek mythology) in Literature. 7. Oedipus (Greek mythology) in literature. I. Title: Sophocles' Oedipus Trilogy. II. Higgins, Regina Kirby. III. Title.

PA4413.O7 H54 2000
882'.01--dc21   00–039692
                                                              CIP

Table of Contents

How to Use This Book

This CliffsNotes study guide on Sophocles' *Oedipus Trilogy* supplements the original literary work, giving you background information about the playwright, an introduction to the work, a graphical character map, critical commentaries, expanded glossaries, and a comprehensive index, all for you to use as an educational tool that will allow you to better understand the *Oedipus Trilogy*. This study guide was written with the assumption that you have read the *Oedipus Trilogy*. Reading a literary work doesn't mean that you immediately grasp the major themes and devices used by the playwright; this study guide will help supplement your reading to be sure you get all you can from Sophocles' *Oedipus Trilogy*. CliffsNotes Review tests your comprehension of the original text and reinforces learning with questions and answers, practice projects, and more. For further information on Sophocles and the *Oedipus Trilogy*, check out the CliffsNotes Resource Center.

CliffsNotes provides the following icons to highlight essential elements of particular interest:

Reveals the underlying themes in the work.

Helps you to more easily relate to or discover the depth of a character.

Uncovers elements such as setting, atmosphere, mystery, passion, violence, irony, symbolism, tragedy, foreshadowing, and satire.

Enables you to appreciate the nuances of words and phrases.

Don't Miss Our Web Site

Discover classic literature as well as modern-day treasures by visiting the CliffsNotes Web site at www.cliffsnotes.com. You can obtain a quick download of a CliffsNotes title, purchase a title in print form, browse our catalog, or view online samples.

You'll also find interactive tools that are fun and informative, links to interesting Web sites, tips, articles, and additional resources to help you, not only for literature, but for test prep, finance, careers, computers, and the Internet too. See you at www.cliffsnotes.com!

LIFE AND BACKGROUND OF THE PLAYWRIGHT

The following abbreviated biography of Sophocles is provided so that you might become more familiar with his life and the historical times that possibly influenced his writing. Read this Life and Background of the Playwright section and recall it when reading Sophocles' *Oedipus Trilogy*, thinking of any thematic relationship between Sophocles' work and his life.

Personal Background

Information about Sophocles' life is at best sketchy and incomplete, but some important details survive. Most of what scholars know about the playwright comes from two sources: the *Suda Lexicon*, a tenth-century Greek dictionary, and the anonymous *Sophocles: His Life and Works*, an undated manuscript found in the thirteenth century.

Early Years

Sophocles was born about 496 B.C. at Colonus, a village just outside Athens, Greece. His father, Sophillus, was a wealthy weapons-maker and a leading citizen. Both birth and wealth, then, set Sophocles apart as someone likely to play an important role in Athenian society.

Education

Like other Greek boys from wealthy families, Sophocles studied poetry, music, dancing, and gymnastics—subjects regarded as the basis of a well-rounded education for a citizen. His early schooling prepared him to serve as a leader in all aspects of public life, including the military, foreign policy, and the arts.

The young Sophocles showed great skill at music and dancing. In fact, at age 15, he won the great honor of leading the boys' chorus in the victory *paean* (joyful song) celebrating the Athenian naval victory over the Persians at the battle of Salamis. This achievement foreshadowed the leadership role Sophocles would have in society, both as an active member of the government and as an influence on Greek arts.

Sophocles lived during the Classical Period (500 to 400 B.C.), a time of transition for Greece, when political and cultural events were changing and shaping Athenian culture. As a dramatist, Sophocles played an important part in this creation of a civilization, which included looking backward to ancient traditions and the first epic poetry of Greece, written by Homer. His great Greek epics *The Odyssey* and *The Iliad* profoundly influenced Sophocles. An anonymous biographer of the time called him "the pupil of Homer"—suggesting that Sophocles' great power came to him from the greatest of Greek poets.

Sophocles probably also studied under the Greek playwright Aeschylus. If so, then Sophocles' first dramatic success had a very personal significance. In 468 B.C., his play *Triptolemus* took first prize for tragedy, while Aeschylus' play came in second.

Public Service

Over many years, Sophocles actively participated in Athenian political and cultural life, often in positions of great responsibility. Besides his contributions as playwright, Sophocles served as a diplomat, general, and even a priest of Alscepius, a minor god of healing. While some of his public service may seem beyond his professional experience as a dramatist, Athenian democracy nevertheless demanded that its citizens take part in all aspects of government.

In 443 B.C., the great Athenian leader Pericles chose Sophocles to be treasurer of the Delian Confederation. As *Hellenotamias*—his official title—Sophocles collected taxes from the states under the control of Athens. In effect, he represented the power of the entire Athenian empire in his office, and the funds he collected bolstered Athenian glory at home and around the Mediterranean.

In 440 B.C., Sophocles served as a general in the siege of Samos, an island that challenged the authority of Athens. He may have served another term as a general in either 426 B.C. or 415 B.C., and he later took part in a special commission to investigate the Athenian military defeat in Sicily in 413 B.C. During the crucial Peloponnesian War, Sophocles conducted negotiations with Athenian allies.

Despite all his public service, though, Sophocles remained first and last a dramatist. His death in 406 B.C. inspired a national cult that worshipped him as a cultural hero at a shrine dedicated to his memory.

Literary Writing

Athens in the fifth century B.C. was a golden age of drama for Greece and the world. For Sophocles to emerge as the most popular playwright among his contemporaries—the older Aeschylus and the younger Euripides—attests to his genius for moving audiences with powerful poetry and stagecraft.

Sophocles wrote more than 120 plays, but only seven complete tragedies survive. Of the rest, only some titles and fragments remain. As late as 1907, a papyrus with several hundred lines of a Sophoclean play called *The Ichneutae* turned up in Egypt.

Perhaps someday other lost plays will come to light, although the prospect seems unlikely. But for now, Sophocles' modern reputation rests on the seven surviving plays: *Ajax*, *Antigone*, *Electra*, *Oedipus the King*, *The Trachinae*, *Philoctetes*, and *Oedipus at Colonus*.

Originally produced around 445 B.C., *Ajax* tells the story of the legendary Trojan War hero who is driven mad by the vengeful goddess Athena. In *Antigone* (440 B.C.), Sophocles dramatizes a tragic conflict between human and divine law in the story of Oedipus' daughter and King Creon. *Electra* (440 B.C.) takes for its subject the revenge of Agamemnon's children on their father's killers.

Oedipus the King (430 B.C.), generally regarded as Sophocles' masterpiece, presents the myth of Oedipus, the man fated to kill his father and marry his mother. Sophocles dramatizes the story of the death of Hercules in *The Trachinae* (413 B.C.) and returns to the subject of the Trojan War in *Philoctetes* (410 B.C.). Sophocles' last work, *Oedipus at Colonus*, presents the death of Oedipus; it was produced in 401 B.C., five years after the playwright's own death.

Of all the surviving plays, the tragedies of the Oedipus Trilogy— *Oedipus the King*, *Oedipus at Colonus*, and *Antigone*—are the best known and most often produced. Although all three plays are part of the same story, Sophocles did not create them to be performed as a single theatrical production. Instead, the three tragedies represent separate dramas on related subjects.

Many people choose to read the plays of the Oedipus Trilogy in the chronological order of the story—*Oedipus the King*, *Oedipus at Colonus*, *Antigone*—while others prefer the order in which Sophocles wrote them—*Antigone*, *Oedipus the King*, *Oedipus at Colonus*. In any order, readers will note the unique qualities in each drama, especially the important differences in character and tone.

In his *Poetics*, Aristotle writes that the purpose of tragedy is to arouse pity and fear in the audience, and so create a catharsis—or cleansing of emotions—that will enlighten people about life and fate. Each of the plays of the Oedipus Trilogy achieves this catharsis that Aristotle defined as the hallmark of all tragedy.

Honors and Awards

Athens held a dramatic competition every year, at the Festival of Dionysus. At this time, three playwrights would each present a *tetralogy*—four tragedies as well as a "satyr play," a kind of short, rough comedy—on three successive days. At the end of the festival, ten judges would award first, second, and third prizes for the best drama. The prize itself is not known, although it was probably money and a symbol of some sort; but the true glory of winning first place was the approval of the Athenian public.

Sophocles won first prize at the Festival of Dionysus 18 times, frequently over such competitors as Aeschylus and Euripides. Some of Sophocles' plays won second prize—*Oedipus the King*, for example—but none ever came in third. Year after year, Sophocles' tragedies gained recognition as among the best dramas written at a time when competition was at its highest.

Perhaps Sophocles' greatest achievement is his enduring popularity as a dramatist. The fact that his works are studied today, approximately 2,400 years after they were written, is a testament to the power of his words and the impact those stories have on current culture.

INTRODUCTION TO THE PLAYS

The following Introduction section is provided solely as an educational tool and is not meant to replace the experience of your reading the work. Read the Introduction and A Brief Synopsis to enhance your understanding of the work and to prepare yourself for the critical thinking that should take place whenever you read any work of fiction or non-fiction. Keep the List of Characters and Character Map at hand so that as you read the original literary work, if you encounter a character about whom you're uncertain, you can refer to the List of Characters and Character Map to refresh your memory.

Historical Background

The Athens Sophocles knew was a small place—a *polis*, one of the self-governing city-states on the Greek peninsula—but it held within it the emerging life of democracy, philosophy, and theater. Socrates, Plato, and Aristotle wrote and taught in Athens, and their ideas gave birth to Western philosophy. Here, too, democracy took root and flourished, with a government ruled entirely by and for its citizens.

During the fifth century B.C., Athens presided as the richest and most advanced of all the city-states. Its army and navy dominated the Aegean after the defeat of the Persians, and the tribute money offered to the conquering Athenians built the Acropolis, site of the Parthenon, as well as the public buildings that housed and glorified Athenian democracy. The wealth of Athens also assured regular public art and entertainment, most notably the Festival of Dionysus, where Sophocles produced his tragedies.

In the fifth century, Athens had reached the height of its development, but Athenians were vulnerable, too. Their land, like most of Greece, was rocky and dry, yielding little food. Athenians often fought neighboring city-states for farmland or cattle. They sought to solve their agricultural problems by reaching outward to more fertile lands through their conquering army and navy forces. Military skill and luck kept Athens wealthy for a time, but the rival city-state Sparta pressed for dominance during the long Peloponnesian War (431– 404 B.C.). By the end of the fifth century, Sparta had starved Athens into submission, and the power of the great city-state ended.

Greek Theater and Its Development

Sophocles' Oedipus Trilogy forms part of a theater tradition that encompasses much more than just entertainment. In fifth century B.C., Athens theater represented an essential public experience—at once social, political, and religious.

For Athenians, theater served as an expression of public unity. Ancient Greek myth—the theme of most tragedies—not only touched members of the audience individually, but drew them together as well. The dramatization of stories from a shared heritage helped to nurture and preserve a cultural identity through times of hardship and war.

But beyond its social and political importance, Greek drama also held a religious significance that made it a sacred art. Originally, the

Greek theater tradition emerged from a long history of choral performance in celebration of the god Dionysus.

The Festival of Dionysus—whose high point was a dramatic competition—served as a ritual to honor the god of wine and fertility and to ask his blessing on the land. To attend the theater, then, was a religious duty and the responsibility of all pious citizens.

Drama began, the Greeks say, when the writer and producer Thespis separated one man from the chorus and gave him some lines to speak by himself. In 534 B.C., records show that this same Thespis produced the first tragedy at the Festival of Dionysus. From then on, plays with actors and a chorus formed the basis of Greek dramatic performances.

The actual theater itself was simple, yet imposing. Actors performed in the open air, while the audience—perhaps 15,000 people—sat in seats built in rows on the side of a hill. The stage was a bare floor with a wooden building (called the *skene*) behind it. The front of the skene might be painted to suggest the location of the action, but its most practical purpose was to offer a place where actors could make their entrances and exits.

In Greek theater, the actors were all male, playing both men and women in long robes with masks that depicted their characters. Their acting was stylized, with wide gestures and movements to represent emotion or reaction. The most important quality for an actor was a strong, expressive voice because chanted poetry remained the focus of dramatic art.

The simplicity of production emphasized what Greeks valued most about drama—poetic language, music, and evocative movement by the actors and chorus in telling the story. Within this simple framework, dramatists found many opportunities for innovation and embellishment. Aeschylus, for example, introduced two actors, and used the chorus to reflect emotions and to serve as a bridge between the audience and the story.

Later, Sophocles introduced painted scenery, an addition that brought a touch of realism to the bare Greek stage. He also changed the music for the chorus, whose size swelled from twelve to fifteen members. Most important, perhaps, Sophocles increased the number of actors from two to three—a change that greatly increased the possibility for interaction and conflict between characters on stage.

The Oedipus Myth

Like other dramatists of his time, Sophocles wrote his plays as theatrical interpretations of the well-known myths of Greek culture—an imaginative national history that grew through centuries. Sophocles and his contemporaries particularly celebrated the mythic heroes of the Trojan War, characters who appear in Homer's *Iliad* and *Odyssey*.

The myth of Oedipus—which also appears briefly in Homer—represents the story of a man's doomed attempt to outwit fate. Sophocles' tragedy dramatizes Oedipus' painful discovery of his true identity, and the despairing violence the truth unleashes in him.

Warned by the oracle at Delphi that their son will kill his father, King Laius and Queen Jocasta of Thebes try to prevent this tragic destiny. Laius pierces his son's feet and gives him to a shepherd with instructions to leave the baby in the mountains to die. But pitying the child, the shepherd gives him to a herdsman, who takes the baby far from Thebes to Corinth. There, the herdsman presents the child to his own king and queen, who are childless. Without knowing the baby's identity, the royal couple adopt the child and name him Oedipus ("swollen-foot").

Oedipus grows up as a prince of Corinth, but hears troubling stories that the king is not his real father. When he travels to Delphi to consult the oracle, Oedipus learns the prophecy of his fate, that he will kill his father and marry his mother. Horrified, he determines to avoid his terrible destiny by never returning home.

Near Thebes, Oedipus encounters an old man in a chariot with his attendants. When the old man insults and strikes him in anger, Oedipus kills the man and his servants. The old man, of course, is Oedipus' father, Laius, but Oedipus does not realize this.

Outside Thebes, Oedipus meets the monstrous Sphinx, who has been terrorizing the countryside. The Sphinx challenges Oedipus with her riddle: "What goes on four feet at dawn, two at noon, and three at evening?" Oedipus responds with the right answer ("A man") and kills the monster.

The Theban people proclaim him a hero, and when they learn that Laius has been killed, apparently by a band of robbers, they accept Oedipus as their king. Oedipus marries Jocasta, and they have four children. Thus, despite all his efforts to prevent it, Oedipus fulfills the dreadful prophecy.

Dramatic Irony

Since everyone knew the myth, Sophocles' play contained no plot surprises for his audience. Instead, the tragedy held their interest through new interpretation, poetic language, and, most especially, dramatic irony.

Dramatic irony arises from the difference between what an audience knows and what the characters on stage know. In *Oedipus the King*, for example, everyone in the audience knows from the beginning that Oedipus has killed his father and married his mother. The tension of the play, then, develops from Oedipus' slow but inevitable progress toward this terrible self-knowledge.

Watching Oedipus' fate unfold, the audience identifies with the hero, sharing vicariously in the horror of the reversal he suffers and acknowledging the power of destiny. By connecting with the audience, Sophocles has achieved the catharsis that Aristotle thought was so important. In accomplishing this dramatic feat, Aristotle declares, Sophocles' *Oedipus the King* stands as the greatest tragedy ever written.

Character Map

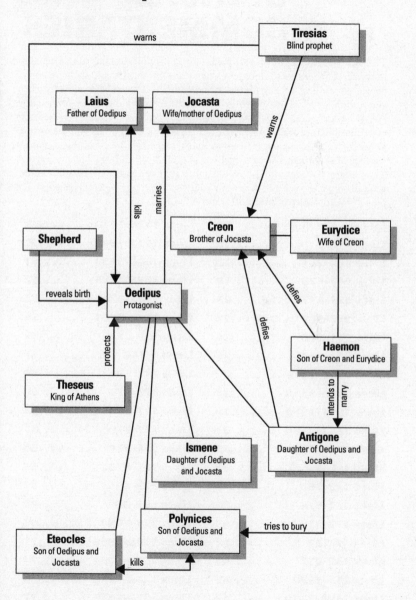

CRITICAL COMMENTARIES

The sections that follow provide great tools for supplementing your reading of the *Oedipus Trilogy*. First, in order to enhance your understanding of and enjoyment from reading, we provide quick summaries in case you have difficulty when you read the original literary work. Each summary is followed by commentary: literary devices, character analyses, themes, and so on. Keep in mind that the interpretations here are solely those of the author of this study guide and are used to jumpstart your thinking about the work. No single interpretation of a complex work like the *Oedipus Trilogy* is infallible or exhaustive, and you'll likely find that you interpret portions of the work differently from the author of this study guide. Read the original work and determine your own interpretations, referring to these Notes for supplemental meanings only.

Oedipus the King

A Brief Synopsis

Oedipus the King unfolds as a murder mystery, a political thriller, and a psychological whodunit. Throughout this mythic story of patricide and incest, Sophocles emphasizes the irony of a man determined to track down, expose, and punish an assassin, who turns out to be himself.

As the play opens, the citizens of Thebes beg their king, Oedipus, to lift the plague that threatens to destroy the city. Oedipus has already sent his brother-in-law, Creon, to the oracle to learn what to do.

On his return, Creon announces that the oracle instructs them to find the murderer of Laius, the king who ruled Thebes before Oedipus. The discovery and punishment of the murderer will end the plague. At once, Oedipus sets about to solve the murder.

Summoned by the king, the blind prophet Tiresias at first refuses to speak, but finally accuses Oedipus himself of killing Laius. Oedipus mocks and rejects the prophet angrily, ordering him to leave, but not before Tiresias hints darkly of an incestuous marriage and a future of blindness, infamy, and wandering.

Oedipus attempts to gain advice from Jocasta, the queen; she encourages him to ignore prophecies, explaining that a prophet once told her that Laius, her husband, would die at the hands of their son. According to Jocasta, the prophecy did not come true because the baby died, abandoned, and Laius himself was killed by a band of robbers at a crossroads.

Oedipus becomes distressed by Jocasta's remarks because just before he came to Thebes he killed a man who resembled Laius at a crossroads. To learn the truth, Oedipus sends for the only living witness to the murder, a shepherd.

Another worry haunts Oedipus. As a young man, he learned from an oracle that he was fated to kill his father and marry his mother. Fear of the prophecy drove him from his home in Corinth and brought him ultimately to Thebes. Again, Jocasta advises him not to worry about prophecies.

Oedipus finds out from a messenger that Polybus, king of Corinth, Oedipus' father, has died of old age. Jocasta rejoices—surely this is proof that the prophecy Oedipus heard is worthless. Still, Oedipus worries about fulfilling the prophecy with his mother, Merope, a concern Jocasta dismisses.

Overhearing, the messenger offers what he believes will be cheering news. Polybus and Merope are not Oedipus' real parents. In fact, the messenger himself gave Oedipus to the royal couple when a shepherd offered him an abandoned baby from the house of Laius.

Oedipus becomes determined to track down the shepherd and learn the truth of his birth. Suddenly terrified, Jocasta begs him to stop, and then runs off to the palace, wild with grief.

Confident that the worst he can hear is a tale of his lowly birth, Oedipus eagerly awaits the shepherd. At first the shepherd refuses to speak, but under threat of death he tells what he knows—Oedipus is actually the son of Laius and Jocasta.

And so, despite his precautions, the prophecy that Oedipus dreaded has actually come true. Realizing that he has killed his father and married his mother, Oedipus is agonized by his fate.

Rushing into the palace, Oedipus finds that the queen has killed herself. Tortured, frenzied, Oedipus takes the pins from her gown and rakes out his eyes, so that he can no longer look upon the misery he has caused. Now blinded and disgraced, Oedipus begs Creon to kill him, but as the play concludes, he quietly submits to Creon's leadership, and humbly awaits the oracle that will determine whether he will stay in Thebes or be cast out forever.

List of Characters

Oedipus King of Thebes. As a young man, he saved the city of Thebes by solving the riddle of the Sphinx and destroying the monster. He now sets about finding the murderer of the former king Laius to save Thebes from plague.

Creon The second-in-command in Thebes, brother-in-law of Oedipus. He is Oedipus' trusted advisor, selected to go to the oracle at Delphi to seek the Apollo's advice in saving the city from plague.

Tiresias A blind prophet who has guided the kings of Thebes with his advice and counsel.

Jocasta Queen of Thebes, wife of Oedipus. She was the widow of Thebes' former king, Laius, and married Oedipus when he saved the city from the Sphinx.

A Messenger from Corinth A man bringing news of the royal family to Oedipus.

A Shepherd A herder from the nearby mountains, who once served in the house of Laius.

A Messenger A man who comes from the palace to announce the death of the queen and the blinding of Oedipus.

Antigone and Ismene Oedipus' young daughters.

Chorus A group of Theban elders, and their Leader, who comment on the events of the drama and react to its tragic progression.

Lines 1-168

Summary

As the play opens, Oedipus, king of Thebes, receives a group of citizens led by an old priest. The priest describes the plague that is destroying the city—a blight on the land causing famine and sickness. Recalling Oedipus' early triumph over the Sphinx, the priest begs the king to save Thebes once more.

Oedipus expresses his sympathy and concern, and announces that he has already sent his brother-in-law Creon to the oracle in an effort to end the plague. As Oedipus speaks, Creon returns with the oracle's message: The plague will end when the murderer of Laius (the former King) is killed or banished.

Oedipus immediately swears to take action to find the murderer and save the city.

Commentary

Literary Device

The first scene presents the problem of the play and indicates the direction of the tragedy to follow. Note especially the dramatic irony of Oedipus' determination to find and punish the murderer of Laius. Sophocles' audience already knows that Oedipus is himself the murderer, but the characters onstage have no idea of the truth.

The oracle—and Oedipus himself—identify the king with the land, so that calamity or corruption in the king causes famine in his domain. This principle existed in many ancient cultures. In some early societies, a famine or pestilence on the land was enough to arouse people to kill their king and choose another—hopefully purer— ruler whose ascent to power could restore the fertility of the land.

The "wasteland" of Thebes—with its hunger, disease, and death—must therefore be the responsibility of the king. Oedipus takes up the challenge, believing he can purge the land by punishing another—unconscious that he himself is the source of corruption.

Character Insight

In this first scene, Oedipus seems outwardly the ideal king, revealing his intelligence, responsibility, and energy—attributes that Athenians prized as their own particular virtues. But his overly eager insistence that Creon announce the oracle's words publicly betrays a certain arrogance about his abilities.

As the play unfolds, then, both Oedipus' virtues and his weaknesses will lead to his ultimate downfall. The audience can see that Oedipus' sense of responsibility for his city-state drives his search for the truth, and because of this the hero gains sympathy—even when he is at his most arrogant, and especially at his fall from power.

Glossary

Here and in the following glossary sections, difficult words and phrases, as well as allusions and historical references are explained.

Thebes chief city of ancient Boeotia, in eastern central Greece. Here, the location of the tragedy.

Zeus the chief deity of Greek mythology, son of Chronus and Rhea and husband of Hera.

Athena the goddess of wisdom, skills, and warfare.

Apollo the god of music, poetry, prophecy, and medicine in Greek and Roman mythology. Here, Apollo is most important as the source of the prophecies of the oracle.

Cadmus a Phoenician prince and founder of Thebes; he kills a dragon and sows its teeth, from which many armed men rise, fighting each other, until only five are left to help him build the city.

Sphinx a winged monster with a lion's body and the head and breasts of a woman. Here, the monster who plagued Thebes by devouring anyone who could not answer her riddle.

Delphi a town in ancient Phocis, on the slopes of Mount Parnassus; seat of the famous ancient oracle of Apollo.

oracle among the ancient Greeks and Romans, the place where or the medium by which deities were consulted. Also, the revelation or response of a medium or priest.

Lines 169–244

Summary

The chorus chants a prayer to the gods Zeus, Apollo, Athena, and Artemis, describing the horrors of the Theban plague. In the name of the people, they beg for deliverance from the gods, but worry about the sacrifice that may be demanded in return.

Commentary

At this point, the chorus takes over the stage, providing a break in the action as they reflect the fear and foreboding implicit in the unfolding drama.

Most practically, this chanting denotes the passage of time, from Oedipus' command to assemble all the Thebans to their appearance before the palace in the next scene. The theme of the chorus—the suffering of Thebes—also develops in detail the reality of the plague, which has been discussed only in general terms so far. The poetic repetition— "Death / so many deaths, numberless deaths on deaths" (203–204)— arouses pity in the audience, as does the chorus' plaintive plea for help from the gods.

Literary
Device

The chorus' anxiety about the price of deliverance also continues the dramatic irony begun in the first scene, foreshadowing the tragedy's climax, the disgrace and downfall of Oedipus.

Glossary

Delos small island in the Aegean, legendary birthplace of Artemis and Apollo.

Artemis the goddess of the moon, wild animals, and hunting in Greek mythology. She is the twin sister of Apollo.

Muses the nine goddesses who preside over literature and the arts and sciences: Calliope, Clio, Euterpe, Melpomene, Terpsichore, Erato, Polyhymnia, Urania, and Thalia.

Lines 245–526

Summary

With the people of Thebes assembled before him, Oedipus calls upon anyone who knows the murderer of Laius to come forward with the truth. As an incentive, the king promises leniency—exile, not death—to the murderer and a reward to anyone providing information. When no one steps forward, Oedipus curses the murderer and anyone who shelters him—including himself.

The blind prophet Tiresias arrives, reluctantly obeying Oedipus' summons. The king asks for Tiresias' help in finding the murderer, but the prophet refuses. Furious, Oedipus accuses Tiresias of taking part in the murder. In response, Tiresias states flatly that Oedipus himself murdered Laius.

The quest for truth collapses into a battle of wits and words, with Oedipus bragging of his victory over the Sphinx instead of pursuing the murderer of Laius. In a rage, Oedipus declares that Tiresias and Creon must be plotting against him. Tiresias replies with dark hints of Oedipus' corruption and his fate. At last, the furious Oedipus orders Tiresias away.

Commentary

Literary Device

Oedipus' address to the people of Thebes offers yet another opportunity for dramatic irony. Describing himself as "a stranger to the story" (248) of the king's murder, Oedipus nevertheless declares that he will fight for Laius "as if he were my father" (301).

Theme

The double identity of Oedipus as both son and murderer of Laius reverberates through this episode, especially in the revelations of Tiresias. The blind prophet's clear assertion that Oedipus is the murderer, as well as his subtler references to Oedipus' marriage, should end all suspense in the drama. And yet the tension heightens when the prophecy evokes Oedipus' fury, leading to the angry confrontation between the prophet and the king.

As a prophet who is both blind and clairvoyant, Tiresias represents the ambiguous nature of all spiritual power. Prophecies, like the words of the oracle, tend to be apparent only in hindsight. But Tiresias' words—". . . you are the murderer you hunt." (413)—are uncompromising, and Oedipus' angry refusal to accept them constitutes a rejection of the prophetic power. Sophocles' audience would have understood immediately that Oedipus was rejecting a long-respected conservative tradition in the Greek city-states.

The ridicule of the prophet and his prophecy reflects a change in Athens during the fifth century B.C., when the proponents of reason began to challenge the authority of spiritual power. Sophocles expresses his own conservative views on prophecy by setting up the double irony of a blind man who can see the future and a seeing man who is nevertheless blind to his own past and present—blind even to his own identity.

Literary Device

Oedipus' metaphorical blindness to the truth, intensified by his anger, provides further dramatic irony, while foreshadowing the king's literal blindness at the end of the drama. Another ironic twist emerges when Oedipus blames Creon for scheming with Tiresias in an attempt to overthrow him and steal his crown. The king cannot guess that as events turn, Creon will succeed him and he will have to beg his fate from Creon.

Glossary

Labdacus, Polydorus, and Agenor the ancestors of Laius, the former king of Thebes, and of Oedipus, his son.

infamy disgrace, dishonor.

Cithaeron the mountain range between Thebes and Corinth. Here, the place where Oedipus was abandoned.

Lines 527-572

Summary

In this ode, the chorus wonders at the prophet's accusation that Oedipus is the murderer of Laius. As loyal subjects, they are horrified and confused. Still, they will stand by their king unless the charges are proved.

Commentary

Theme

The ode continues the theme of belief in spiritual power contrasted with reason and everyday common sense. The opening ritually glorifies the Olympian gods, especially their power to reveal truth and destroy evil. The murderer, the chorus warns, will be hunted down by the gods through their oracle, who will descend upon the guilty like "dark wings beating around him shrieking doom" (548).

Style & Language

But the chorus does not trust prophecy completely, and so the image turns around. In the second half of the ode, the chorus itself feels "wings of dark foreboding beating" (552) around them because the prophecy implicates their king. The moment tests the peoples' faith in both the gods and the state, forcing them to choose belief or reason. Conflicted and confused, they come to an uneasy compromise—revere the god, but demand proof of his prophet. This solution allows the chorus to remain loyal to Oedipus while keeping open to conviction on his guilt.

Glossary

Parnassus mountain in central Greece, sacred to Apollo.

Polybus king of Corinth, Oedipus' adoptive father.

Lines 573–953

Summary

The scene opens with Creon's denial of plotting against Oedipus. When Oedipus angrily repeats his charges, Creon again denies it, arguing rationally that he has no motivation to usurp the throne. The wrangling stops when Jocasta—the queen and Creon's sister—divides the men, sending Creon home.

Oedipus continues to complain of Creon's charge (through Tiresias) that he himself killed Laius. When Jocasta hears that the charge comes from a prophet, she dismisses it immediately. No one can see the future, she insists. As proof, she offers the story of a prophecy that her son would kill her husband, a fate avoided when Laius abandoned the child on a mountain.

After Oedipus learns the details of Laius' death, he begins to worry that he is indeed the murderer. Jocasta, however, reminds him that Laius died at the hands of many men, not one. Nevertheless, Oedipus asks that the only living witness to the murderer—a shepherd—be brought to him for questioning.

Commentary

This scene marks the change in the play from a simple detective story to psychological drama. From now on, the problem of the play will be not only who killed Laius, but also what can people know of one another and themselves, and how can they know it.

Despite his rejection of Tiresias, Oedipus does believe in the power of prophecy, as he confesses to Jocasta. Oedipus recalls two disturbing revelations—one from an oracle, the other from a drunken man—that make him doubt himself. Note that the drunken man's railings complement and confirm the oracle's message about Oedipus' fate. At the Festival of Dionysus—the god of wine—such a telling detail would be regarded as a tribute.

Jocasta, in contrast to Oedipus, rejects the power of prophecy, citing as proof her own experience with the oracle who predicted that her son would kill her husband. But as she takes Oedipus through a rational explanation of why the prophecy turned out to be false, she unexpectedly jogs his memory. Paradoxically, then, Jocasta's skepticism brings Oedipus to the suspicion that perhaps the prophet is right after all— and that he is the murderer of Laius.

Glossary

hearsay something one has heard, but does not know to be true.

Phocis ancient region in central Greece. Here, the place where Oedipus killed Laius.

Daulia area north of the road from Thebes to Delphi.

Dorian a native of Doris, a member of one of the four main peoples of ancient Greece. Here, the term describes Oedipus' adoptive mother.

Corinth ancient city of Greece located in the north east Peloponnesus, in the islands off central Greece. A city noted for its luxury, here, it is the home of Oedipus after his adoption.

Lines 954-996

Summary

The chorus glorifies the gods and destiny, rejecting human pride.

Commentary

In the ode, the chorus reflects Oedipus' emerging belief that the prophecies may be correct and that the gods will tear down the proud. Note especially the nostalgic tone of the conclusion, when the chorus laments the erosion of respect for prophecy.

Glossary

Abae a place north of Thebes, where an oracle of Apollo presided.

Olympia a plain in ancient Elis, in the western Peloponnesus; also the location of a temple to Apollo and an oracle.

Lines 997-1194

Summary

As Jocasta makes a sacrifice to Apollo, a messenger arrives to announce the death of Polybus. Oedipus rejoices at the news that the father he feared he would kill has died of natural causes, but he continues to worry about the prophecy because his mother still lives.

Overhearing Oedipus, the messenger tells the king that he has nothing to worry about, since Polybus and Merope were not his real parents. This news stuns Oedipus, and he awaits the shepherd to learn the truth of his birth.

Jocasta now realizes that Oedipus is the baby she and Laius abandoned, and that the prophecy has come true. She begs Oedipus to stop his inquiry, but he refuses, and she runs into the palace screaming.

Commentary

This scene turns on multiple ironies as Oedipus draws closer to the revelation of his birth. For example, the messenger from Corinth brings conflicting news—your father is dead, he tells Oedipus, but he is not your father.

Even the opening ritual of the episode involves irony. Despite her earlier skepticism, Jocasta burns incense to Apollo. Ironically, she implores Apollo—the source of this prophetic truth and the god of prophecy—to release Oedipus from his fears about the very prophecy Apollo himself has given.

Yet the news from the messenger returns Jocasta to her original views on prophecy. She even brushes aside Oedipus' continuing anxiety about his mother with the impious suggestion that he "live at random" (1072), completely oblivious to Apollo's warning. Her bravado is shattered, however, as the scene unfolds and she realizes that Oedipus is, in fact, the child she abandoned.

Meanwhile, Apollo seems to have answered Jocasta's prayer. With the terrible truth pressing in on him, Oedipus calls triumphantly for the shepherd who will tell him everything. At this moment, Oedipus revels in the kind of pride that always precedes the downfall of a tragic hero. He seems proud even in his (mistaken) belief that he is the son of a shepherd and the goddess Chance, "the giver of all good things" (1189). In calling Chance a goddess, Oedipus follows Jocasta's questionable advice to acknowledge that "chance rules our lives" (1070).

By now, the truth of Oedipus' birth is practically unavoidable, but the fact that he still cannot guess it—and that Jocasta has only now realized it—would not have seemed strange to Sophocles' audience. Sophocles meant for the audience to suspend their disbelief, and let the tragedy unfold according to its own conventions. Readers today should do the same.

Lines 1195-1214

Summary

The chorus sings a joyful ode to Mount Cithaeron, where Oedipus was found. They wonder if some god or goddess actually gave their king birth.

Commentary

The chorus takes up Oedipus' triumphal declaration that he is the son of Chance and speculates about his mysterious birth. Perhaps, the chorus suggests, he is really the son of Pan, or Dionysus, or even Apollo himself.

Relieved to hear the possibility of something great and glorious about their beloved king after Tiresias' terrible pronouncements, the chorus jumps on the uncertainty of Oedipus' birth and expands on his vision. The enthusiasm of the chorus elevates Oedipus to divine proportions. This hopeful viewpoint sets the stage for Oedipus to fall from even greater heights as a tragic hero.

Glossary

Pan the god of fields, forests, wild animals, and shepherds.

Hermes the god who is herald and messenger of the other gods.

Dionysus the god of wine and revelry.

Lines 1215-1310

Summary

The shepherd arrives but resists telling what he knows. Only when Oedipus threatens violence does the shepherd reveal that long ago he disobeyed his orders and saved the baby out of pity. And, finally, he admits that the baby was the son of Laius and Jocasta.

With this news, Oedipus realizes that he has murdered his father and married his mother. Horrified by his crimes, Oedipus rushes wildly into the palace.

Commentary

This is the climax of the play. All previous action has moved toward this point of revelation, and this moment, in turn, will determine the outcome of the play. What remains after this scene is the unimaginable consequence of such terrible knowledge. Knowing what he knows, what will Oedipus do?

Character Insight

Note the energy and determination Oedipus manifests in uncovering the truth of his birth. When the shepherd refuses to speak, Oedipus threatens the man with torture and death. In fact, Oedipus appears to be totally in control of the situation—until the lowly shepherd reveals the truth about him.

The match between a king and a shepherd would seem, in another story, to be a fairly straightforward one. The shepherd would tell the king what he's asked out of fear for his life. But this shepherd knows that what he has to tell may drive the king to violence—probably against him. For this reason and because what he has to say would reveal his part in the plot, he tries to keep the truth to himself.

In his tragic downfall, Oedipus suffers from a very human dilemma. At one moment, he seems all-powerful and in charge of his destiny— but in the next moment he becomes vulnerable and powerless. The audience experiences the pity and terror that leads to catharsis.

Glossary

Arcturus a giant orange star in the constellation Bootes, the bright-
est star in the northern celestial sphere. Here, for the ancient
Greeks, its appearance marked the beginning of the winter season.

Lines 1311-1350

Summary

The chorus laments Oedipus' discovery of his birth, wondering at the king's fall from power and greatness.

Commentary

Just as the previous ode expands on Oedipus' confidence, this ode reflects and magnifies his horror and pain.

Literary Device

The chorus chooses Oedipus as its example of the fragility of human life. Joy, the chorus chants, is an illusion that quickly fades. The glory of Oedipus' victory over the Sphinx is now buried in the infamy of his marriage. The chorus' comment on the uncertainty of life foreshadows its own final lamentation on the power of fate in the last lines of the play.

The chorus also looks to Oedipus as a kind of father—"you gave me life" (1348)—and his disgrace therefore brings shame upon the whole city. The phrase "now you bring down night upon my eyes" (1350) expresses this suffering, while foreshadowing Oedipus' violence against himself at the end of the play.

Glossary

dirge a funeral hymn.

Lines 1351-1684

Summary

A messenger from the palace announces that the queen is dead. He describes the details of the queen's suicide as well as Oedipus' horrifying self-blinding with Jocasta's pins.

Oedipus appears on stage to the horror and pity of the chorus. Questioned about his self-mutilation, Oedipus explains in agony that he has raked out his eyes because he could not look again upon the loved ones he has defiled, especially his daughters Ismene and Antigone.

Oedipus begs Creon—who has assumed authority in Thebes—to have him put to death or banished. Creon says that he will consult the oracle for judgement; in the meantime, he counsels Oedipus to accept obedience. Humbled, Oedipus disappears with Creon into the palace, as the chorus again laments Oedipus' downfall.

Commentary

Driven to madness by the revelation of his unconscious actions, Oedipus' conscious and deliberate self-blinding—a methodical, rhythmic action—seems to serve as his way of taking control of the pain that torments him. The violence empties and exhausts Oedipus' fury, and he accepts his fate by becoming one with it: "I am agony" (1444).

The final resolution, then, is the humbling of the once proud Oedipus—his literal acceptance of his blindness and his submission to another's will. Now the willful king yields to his fate—an uncertain future tarnished by his infamy—as the chorus laments Oedipus' fall from greatness with the warning to "count no man happy till he dies, free of pain at last" (1684).

The Athenians were known throughout the ancient world for their decisive action and determination, but, by definition, no one can withstand the blows of fate, anymore than one can avoid death. Therefore, the pity and terror aroused by Oedipus' tragic fall brings about a catharsis, the realization that the power of fate cannot be overcome by will—even by the will of a king.

Modern readers may wonder why Oedipus' self-mutilation occurs off-stage and is announced by the messenger to the assembled elders (and audience). Greek theater had strict conventions, and one of the strictest involved the depiction of violence. Such action occurred *ob skena*—off-stage—as a matter of tradition. This Greek term later came into English as "obscene," meaning offensive to prevailing notions of decency.

Oedipus at Colonus

A Brief Synopsis

In *Oedipus at Colonus*, Sophocles dramatizes the end of the tragic hero's life and his mythic significance for Athens. During the course of the play, Oedipus undergoes a transformation from an abject beggar, banished from his city because of his sins, into a figure of immense power, capable of extending (or withholding) divine blessings.

As the play opens, Oedipus appears as a blind beggar, banished from Thebes. Oedipus and Antigone, his daughter and guide, learn they have reached Colonus, a city near Athens, and are standing on ground sacred to the Eumenides (another name for the Furies). This discovery causes Oedipus to demand that Theseus, king of Athens, be brought to him. Meanwhile, Oedipus' other daughter, Ismene, arrives from Thebes with the news that Creon and Eteocles, Oedipus' son, want Oedipus to return to Thebes in order to secure his blessing and avoid a harsh fate foretold by the oracle. Oedipus refuses to return, and when Theseus arrives, Oedipus promises him a great blessing for the city if he is allowed to stay, die, and be buried at Colonus.

Theseus pledges his help, and when Creon appears threatening war and holding the daughters hostage for Oedipus' return, the Athenian king drives Creon off and frees the daughters. Shortly after Creon leaves, Oedipus' other son, Polynices, arrives to beg his father's support in his war to regain the Theban throne from his brother and Creon. Oedipus angrily curses Polynices, prophesying that he and his brother Eteocles will die at one another's hand.

Suddenly, Oedipus hears thunder and declares that his death is at hand. He leads Theseus, Ismene, and Antigone into a hidden part of the grove and ritually prepares for death. Only Theseus, however, actually witnesses the end of Oedipus' life.

Since Oedipus' final resting place is at Colonus, Athens receives his blessing and protection, and Thebes earns his curse. At the conclusion of the play, Antigone and Ismene return to Thebes, hoping to avert the war and civil strife.

List of Characters

Oedipus Former king of Thebes, now a blind beggar who wanders from place to place. Considered a pariah because of his sins, Oedipus suffers abuse and rejection everywhere he goes.

Antigone Daughter of Oedipus. She leads her blind father on his travels and serves his needs.

A Citizen of Colonus A passer-by who notices Oedipus and Antigone trespassing on sacred ground.

Ismene Daughter of Oedipus, sister of Antigone. She lives in Thebes and brings her father and sister news while they stay in Colonus.

Theseus King of Athens. He acts as Oedipus' ally by protecting him in Colonus and witnesses his death.

Creon King of Thebes, brother-in-law of Oedipus. Responsible for Oedipus' exile, Creon is now interested in returning the former king to Thebes to avoid a curse.

Polynices Son of Oedipus, brother of Antigone and Ismene. Driven out of Thebes after a power struggle with his brother Eteocles and Creon, he is an exile like his father, and plans to take Thebes by force.

A Messenger A man who tells the elders of the city of Oedipus' death.

Chorus A group of elders of Colonus who confront Oedipus and comment on the unfolding events in the play.

Lines 1-141

Summary

The play opens several years after Oedipus' banishment from Thebes. The aged, blind Oedipus, led by his daughter Antigone, arrives in a sacred grove at Colonus, outside Athens.

Commentary

From his entrance, Oedipus shows a clear change of character from the passionate, willful hero of *Oedipus the King*. Older, worn by years of wandering, Oedipus now accepts his fate with resignation, just as he accepts the scraps he begs with patience and humility.

But Oedipus springs to life with the news that he is sitting in a grove sacred to the Eumenides, the sometimes terrible, sometimes kindly spirits who rule over unavenged crimes, especially within families. Oedipus has reason to believe that the Eumenides have taken pity on him. According to the oracle, this grove will be his resting place. In a wild eagerness for release from his suffering, Oedipus refuses to move, despite a citizen's warning that he is trespassing. In this, he shows the willfulness of the old Oedipus.

His renewed spirit also emerges in his command that the citizen bring Theseus, king of Athens, to the grove to hear what blessings Oedipus might bring the city. Here the old, blind man speaks not only with the authority of a king, but also as a messenger of the gods themselves.

Glossary

Furies the three terrible female spirits with snaky hair who punish the doers of unavenged crimes.

Colonus a village to the north of Athens. Here, the setting for the tragedy.

Thebes chief city of ancient Boeotia, in eastern central Greece. Here, the kingdom that Oedipus once ruled.

Terrible Goddesses another name for the Furies.

Eumenides, the Kindly Ones other names for the Furies.

Poseidon god of the sea and of horses.

Prometheus a Titan who steals fires from heaven for the benefit of mankind; in punishment, Zeus chains him to a rock where a vulture (or eagle) comes each day to eat his liver, which grows back each night.

Theseus the principal hero of Attica, son of Aegeus and king of Athens, famed especially for his killing of the Minotaur. Here, Oedipus' chief ally.

Aegeus a king of Athens who drowns himself when he thinks his son Theseus is dead.

Apollo the god of music, poetry, prophecy, and medicine in Greek and Roman mythology. Here, Apollo is most important as the source of the prophecies of the oracle.

Athena the goddess of wisdom, skills, and warfare.

Lines 142-268

Summary

The chorus of elders enters, searching for the man who trespasses in the sacred grove. Oedipus offers to come out of the sacred precinct if they promise not to harm him, and they agree.

In the conversation that follows, Oedipus reveals his identity. Sympathetic, but still horrified, the elders urge Oedipus to leave town.

Commentary

Style & Language

Note that Sophocles shapes this scene with an emphasis on hurried exchanges and outbursts, expressing the confusion and then the anxiety of the elders of Colonus.

The chorus begins their chant with the energy of pursuit—"Look for the man! Who is he? Where's he hiding?" (142). Later, their exchanges with Oedipus tend to be short and directed, as they shout instructions about where he may sit.

The chorus even peppers Oedipus' retelling of his fate with sudden outbursts. The whole effect of the rapid exchanges quickens the scene, introducing necessary plot summary economically, while also emphasizing that the panicked elders are rushing to judgment of Oedipus out of fear of the gods' fury.

Their final order for Oedipus to leave Colonus, therefore, constitutes a snap decision—one they will think through more carefully over the course of the play.

Glossary

libation the ritual of pouring out wine or oil upon the ground as a sacrifice to a god. Here it refers to the sacrifice that must be made to please the Furies, to whom the grove is sacred.

Laius king of Thebes before his son, Oedipus. Killed by Oedipus before the action of the tragedy Oedipus the King.

Thebes chief city of ancient Boeotia, in eastern central Greece. Here, the city from which Oedipus was banished.

Argos ancient city-state in the northeast Peloponnesus from the seventh century B.C. until the rise of Sparta. Here, the location of Oedipus' son Polynices.

oracle among the ancient Greeks and Romans, the place where or the medium by which deities were consulted. Also, the revelation or response of a medium or priest.

Delphi a town in ancient Phocis, on the slopes of Mount Parnassus; seat of the famous ancient oracle of Apollo.

Lines 269-576

Summary

Oedipus persuades the elders to take no action until Theseus, king of Athens, arrives.

Suddenly Ismene, Oedipus' daughter, enters, having come on horseback from Thebes. She tells Oedipus about his sons, Eteocles and Polynices, who are fighting over Thebes. Ismene also tells her father that the oracle at Delphi has made another prophecy—a curse will fall on the Thebans the day that they stand on Oedipus' tomb.

Ismene warns Oedipus that his sons and Creon know of the prophecy and will try to bring him back to Thebes. They plan to keep Oedipus just outside the city—where he will stay under their control without polluting Thebes—and then leave his body unburied at death.

Oedipus curses his sons and praises his faithful daughters for their sacrifice. He tells the elders that he does not want to return to Thebes, and if they help him, he will give his blessing to Athens. The elders accept his proposal and advise him to make an offering to the Eumenides for trespassing on their ground. Ismene leaves to perform the ritual for her father.

Commentary

Theme

This episode sets up the problem of the play—a family's fight over their father's dead body, even while he still lives.

The conflict in Thebes—Polynices' battle to take the city by force from Creon and Eteocles—arises from the power vacuum created by Oedipus' downfall. The crisis itself is the subject of Aeschylus' play *Seven Against Thebes* (467 B.C.).

Long ago, Creon banished an unwilling Oedipus, and Eteocles and Polynices did nothing to stop Creon or help Oedipus. Now, because of the prophecy, all want him back to avoid the curse. Paradoxically, the Theban curse will be a blessing of victory to those from another city who will offer Oedipus burial. In this, as Ismene points out, Oedipus' fortune as a pariah has been reversed.

Note that Oedipus' present misery as a blind beggar reflects the condition of Athens itself at the end of the fifth century—weakening, under siege, about to accept defeat as the long Peloponnesian War draws to a close. Yet Oedipus refers to Athens as a powerful city, the shelter of all who seek her help. This nostalgic note represents Sophocles' tribute to his once great *polis*.

Note, too, the purification ritual that the elders explain to Oedipus. Such rites were common in ancient Athens, echoing the mysteries of Eleusis, an initiation into the truth of death and eternal life. The ritual also looks forward to Oedipus' transformation upon his death at the end of the play.

Glossary

Zeus the chief deity of Greek mythology, son of Chronus and Rhea and husband of Hera.

Lines 577-616

Summary

When the elders question Oedipus about his past, he at first refuses to answer, but finally consents. He admits his wrongdoing, but insists that he killed his father in self-defense and married his mother in ignorance.

Commentary

The elders here seem strident, even prurient, in their questioning. Their unkindness to the aged, blind beggar deepens the audience's sympathy for Oedipus as he explains his crimes—and his sufferings—from his own point of view.

In essence, this dialogue represents another kind of purification ritual—a painful confession—paralleling the ritual Ismene carries out offstage.

Line 617-761

Summary

When Theseus arrives, he immediately recognizes Oedipus, who is famous for his guilt and suffering. The Athenian king offers the blind beggar his help. Oedipus thanks Theseus and asks to stay in Athens until his death, promising that Athens will be rewarded. He warns that the peace between Athens and Thebes will be ended if Theseus helps him.

Despite this warning, Theseus promises his aid. He grants Oedipus Athenian citizenship, and leaves him under the protection of the elders while he returns to Athens.

Commentary

In his respect for Oedipus and his acknowledgment of the old man's sufferings, Theseus reinforces the sympathetic view of the exiled former king that Oedipus' speeches created in the previous dialogue with the elders. This respectful approach toward Oedipus, in turn, establishes Theseus as a character commanding respect and sympathy. In fact, Oedipus himself praises Theseus, calling the king "so magnanimous, so noble!" (641–642).

This episode includes one of the most famous speeches written by Sophocles (685–712). To Theseus' question about why Thebes and Athens should ever come to war, Oedipus answers with all the authority of his own horrendous experience, describing the instability of life and earthly circumstances.

Glossary

Dionysus the god of wine and revelry.

Great Goddesses here, a term to refer to Demeter, the goddess of agriculture, and her daughter Persephone, the goddess of the underworld and the spring. They are the deities of the Eleusian Mysteries, which granted initiates the hope of life after death.

Cephisus a river of Attica.

Muses the nine goddesses who preside over literature and the arts and sciences: Calliope, Clio, Euterpe, Melpomene, Terpsichore, Erato, Polyhymnia, Urania, and Thalia.

Aphrodite the goddess of love and beauty.

Pelops' broad Dorian island here, a reference to the Peloponnesus, a peninsula forming the southern part of the mainland in Greece.

Lines 762-817

Summary

The chorus sings a lyrical ode praising the natural beauties of the Athenian countryside.

Commentary

Theseus' conferral of citizenship upon Oedipus inspires the elders' celebratory ode to the glories of Athens and its surrounding lands.

Sophocles offers this evocation of natural beauty at a time when Athens was brought low by war, and so the description is of an idyllic place, still fresh from creation. The poetic emphasis is on the divinity that enlivens the landscape. Horses, for instance, represent the power of Poseidon, and olives, the sheltering genius of Athena.

Note, too, that the ode pays particular attention to the narcissus, a flower associated with Demeter and Persephone, who went down among the dead and returned to life. The narcissus is also associated with the Eleusian Mysteries, a ritual of death and rebirth. Again, the reference looks forward to Oedipus' approaching death and his transformation into a spirit with a god's power.

Glossary

Mount of Ares a hill in Athens, the site of the first court of law.

Lines 818-1192

Summary

Creon enters with his attendants and tries to persuade Oedipus to return to Thebes. Oedipus sees through Creon's hypocrisy and recalls the many times in the past when he showed him no pity. Creon has his men seize Antigone and tells Oedipus that Ismene is already a prisoner.

Theseus arrives with his party and takes Creon hostage, reprimanding him for violation of Athenian territory. With Creon as his prisoner, Theseus sends his men to rescue Ismene and Antigone.

Commentary

This scene moves from polite conversation to threats of war, dramatizing the three principals in the play: Oedipus as the suffering victim of his fate, Theseus as the fair-minded decisive leader, and Creon as the duplicitous bully.

When Theseus accuses Creon of unlawful action, Creon justifies himself by citing the many sins committed by Oedipus. Oedipus, in turn, defends himself by insisting that the gods condemned him to his fate. He committed his crimes unknowingly and discovered their significance too late. Creon, however, badgers the old man, knowing full well what he's doing. Anguished, angry, and broken by the blows of destiny and the humiliation of exile, Oedipus nevertheless defends himself. At the very least, he is determined to give the gift of his grave and with it the power of his blessing, to the city he himself chooses Athens.

In response, the elders side with Oedipus, whom they now see as innocent of sin, although cursed by ill fortune. Their change in judgment begins the preparation for Oedipus' apotheosis—elevation to divine status—at the end of the play.

Note, too, that Creon's character in this play contrasts sharply with the reasonable Creon of *Oedipus the King*. In this scene, Creon starts with a hypocritical, duplicitous speech to Oedipus and ends with hostage-taking and threats of war. Creon's transformation from bad to worse contrasts with the transformation of Oedipus, who changes from a reviled man to a figure with god-like powers at the end of the play.

Glossary

unctuous characterized by a smug, smooth pretense of spiritual feeling, fervor or earnestness, as in seeking to persuade; too suave or oily in speech or manner.

Lines 1193-1239

Summary

In excited anticipation, the chorus evokes—and, for a moment, actually dramatizes—the expected battle between Athens and Thebes, ending the ode with a heartfelt prayer to the gods for victory for Athens.

Commentary

At the middle of the choral ode, after a respectful reference to the god Apollo and the goddess Athena, deities of Athens, the chorus breaks into individual voices. Five different men take a role, each speaking as a soldier looking forward to the battle. The long-fought Peloponnesian War, still raging through Greece, brought a special significance to these passages for the audience. The enemy might be at Athens' own gates. Athenians, like the men of the chorus, were filled with hope and terror of the day of battle.

Literary
Device

Note, too, the reference to the Eleusian Mysteries in lines 1198-1202—a foreshadowing of Oedipus' death and transformation.

Glossary

Artemis the goddess of the moon, wild animals, and hunting. She is the twin sister of Apollo.

Lines 1240–1377

Summary

Theseus and his followers return with Antigone and Ismene. A grateful Oedipus steps forward to embrace Theseus, but suddenly restrains himself out of fear that he might defile the Athenian king.

Theseus tells Oedipus that a stranger awaits him at the altar of Poseidon. This stranger from Argos claims to be a kinsman of Oedipus. Oedipus realizes that it is Polynices and refuses to talk with him, but Theseus and Antigone persuade Oedipus to receive him.

Commentary

This scene dramatizes both the political and spiritual consequences of Oedipus' tragedy.

Reunited with Ismene and Antigone, Oedipus seems genuinely happy for the first time. In another play, this might be the ending, but Oedipus' sense of his own defilement undercuts his joy. He restrains his impulse to take Theseus' hand in gratitude, suddenly reminded of his sinful state. Note that although Theseus reassures Oedipus, he does not take his hand.

The arrival of Polynices reminds Oedipus again of the consequences of his sins. Polynices' entrance will bring forward once more the unstable political situation in Thebes that Oedipus grappled with in the scene with Creon.

Literary Device

This is a play full of surprise entrances—the approach of Ismene, Creon's unexpected arrival, and now the appearance of Polynices, whom Theseus describes without even knowing his name. All these surprise arrivals suggest a mystery unfolding toward some ultimate revelation.

Glossary

Aetolia region of ancient Greece, on the Gulf of Corinth.

Arcadia ancient, relatively isolated pastoral region in the central Peloponnesus.

Lines 1378–1410

Summary

The chorus sings an ode on the suffering and grief of old age.

Commentary

Oedipus' old age and approaching death inspire this sad chant, but the ode also includes an acknowledgment of the old man's endurance.

After a long description of life's increasing burdens, the conclusion offers an image of age as a "great headland fronting the north" (1401), a landscape exposed to every kind of harsh weather. Oedipus, by extension, can do nothing but endure the hardships that will come—including the arrival of his son, Polynices, who brings yet another assault on the old man's peace.

Lines 1411–1645

Summary

When Polynices arrives seeking Oedipus' support in his struggle for the Theban throne, Oedipus at first refuses to talk with him. After Polynices makes his argument—namely, that both he and his father have suffered at the hands of Eteocles and Creon and that both will prosper if Polynices' side wins the throne—Oedipus rejects him in fury. Despite his father's curse that the brothers should die at one another's hands and despite Antigone's pleadings to avoid war, Polynices goes back to his troops, ready to storm Thebes.

Commentary

With the arrival of Polynices, two other tragedies intersect with the main story. Polynices' vain attempt to take the throne from Eteocles will end in both the brothers' deaths, a story dramatized in Aeschylus' *Seven Against Thebes*. As in Oedipus' own story, Polynices' fate is foretold; but, unlike his father, he continues to pursue his object—Thebes—in the belief that his fate cannot be fully known or avoided. Antigone's pleas, therefore, do not move him, although Polynices does ask his sister to see to his burial, a request that foreshadows the last tragedy of the Oedipus Trilogy, *Antigone*.

Although Oedipus' wrath recalls his uncontrollable rage at the end of *Oedipus the King* rather than his present wiser and calmer state, to Sophocles' audience, Oedipus' fury is a righteous wrath. The intensity of Oedipus' rage and the brutality of his curse on his son may seem out of bounds to modern readers, but in fifth century Athens, honoring one's parents was a primary duty. Even Polynices himself describes Oedipus' wretched condition and apologizes for neglecting his father. This neglect and Polynices' part in his father's banishment constitute serious offenses.

Lines 1646-1694

Summary

The chorus describes thunder sounding, and Oedipus announces that it is the signal of his approaching death.

Commentary

This choral dialogue suggests a ritual conversation—the elders describing the blasting thunderstorm, appalling to hear, while Oedipus interprets its meaning for them and for the audience.

By this time, purged of his anger, Oedipus speaks in calm, commanding tones. He understands that the culmination of his fate is at hand; he has reached his resting place and will give the gift of his tomb to Athens.

Lines 1695-1765

Summary

Oedipus says that he will lead Theseus, Ismene, and Antigone to his gravesite, where his tomb will be a blessing to Athens.

Commentary

In this episode, Oedipus and Theseus have, in effect, changed roles. Oedipus—once the helpless wanderer begging for shelter—now confidently leads the king who provided him protection into the sacred precinct, where he promises powerful blessings. Oedipus himself points out the irony that he, the blind man, leads the rest.

In yielding the gift of his tomb to Athens—the power that will keep the city safe from Theban attack—Oedipus reminds Theseus of the paradox of eternal life. Though dead, Oedipus will enliven Athens forever. Oedipus' humble request to be remembered is the last onstage speech of the tragic character.

Note especially Oedipus' reference to the Eleusian Mysteries and his insistence upon secrecy. The passage from death to eternal life that he is about to accomplish is a holy mystery, full of awe, power, and dread.

Glossary

dragon's teeth a reference to the legend that the original Thebans sprung up as armed men from dragon's teeth sown by their first king, Cadmus.

Hermes the god who is herald and messenger of the other gods. Here, referred to as the god that will escort Oedipus to the underworld.

Persephone the daughter of Zeus and Demeter, abducted by Hades to be his wife in the lower world. The Queen of Hades.

Lines 1766-1788

Summary

The elders chant a prayer to the gods of the Underworld to receive Oedipus in death.

Commentary

The ode, solemn and stately, implores the god and goddess of the Underworld, Hades and Persephone, to grant Oedipus the justice and the glory that he was denied in life.

The prayer, in effect, reflects the final acknowledgment of the tragic grandeur of the long-suffering Oedipus. From their initial horror, the chorus of elders has now come around to a genuine sympathy and admiration of the tragic figure—a transformation paralleling the catharsis that the audience experiences.

Glossary

Cerberus the three-headed dog guarding the gate of Hades.

Lines 1789-2001

Summary

A messenger arrives, announcing to the elders that Oedipus is dead. After describing the rituals that Oedipus, his daughter, and Theseus performed in preparation, the messenger explains that only Theseus can witness the passing of the tragic hero.

After her father's death, Antigone begs Theseus to take her to the grave. Theseus refuses, explaining that Oedipus wished its location to remain a mystery. Antigone says that she and her sister will return to Thebes, and Theseus promises his protection.

The chorus ends the play with the admonition to stop weeping and trust in the gods.

Commentary

This final scene emphasizes that the play constitutes a drama of transformation of Oedipus from a blind beggar—cast out and reviled as society's ultimate sinner—to a heroic figure, sanctified and at one with the gods. The final mystical scene demonstrates the heroic stature and dignity that one can achieve despite—or perhaps because of—human suffering in an incomprehensible world.

The rituals surrounding the death of Oedipus and Theseus' witnessing of his mysterious passing again recall the Eleusian Mysteries that offered initiates powerful assurances of life after death. As his gift to Athens, Oedipus chooses Theseus alone to witness his death, which allows the king to gain the wisdom of eternal life.

Note that Antigone and Ismene will return to Thebes. In returning home, the two sisters head directly, as if driven by fate, for the events that will unfold as the final tragedy of the Oedipus Trilogy, *Antigone*.

Glossary

Perithous the hero who went with Theseus into the lower world to bring back Persephone.

dirge a funeral hymn.

Antigone

A Brief Synopsis

After the bloody siege of Thebes by Polynices and his allies, the city stands unconquered. Polynices and his brother Eteocles, however, are both dead, killed by each other, according to the curse of Oedipus, their father.

Outside the city gates, Antigone tells Ismene that Creon has ordered that Eteocles, who died defending the city, is to be buried with full honors, while the body of Polynices, the invader, is left to rot. Furthermore, Creon has declared that anyone attempting to bury Polynices shall be publicly stoned to death. Outraged, Antigone reveals to Ismene a plan to bury Polynices in secret, despite Creon's order. When Ismene timidly refuses to defy the king, Antigone angrily rejects her and goes off alone to bury her brother.

Creon discovers that someone has attempted to offer a ritual burial to Polynices and demands that the guilty one be found and brought before him. When he discovers that Antigone, his niece, has defied his order, Creon is furious. Antigone makes an impassioned argument, declaring Creon's order to be against the laws of the gods themselves. Enraged by Antigone's refusal to submit to his authority, Creon declares that she and her sister will be put to death.

Haemon, Creon's son who was to marry Antigone, advises his father to reconsider his decision. The father and son argue, Haemon accusing Creon of arrogance, and Creon accusing Haemon of unmanly weakness in siding with a woman. Haemon leaves in anger, swearing never to return. Without admitting that Haemon may be right, Creon amends his pronouncement on the sisters: Ismene shall live, and Antigone will be sealed in a tomb to die of starvation, rather than stoned to death by the city.

The blind prophet Tiresias warns Creon that the gods disapprove of his leaving Polynices unburied and will punish the king's impiety with the death of his own son. After rejecting Tiresias angrily, Creon reconsiders and decides to bury Polynices and free Antigone.

But Creon's change of heart comes too late. Antigone has hanged herself and Haemon, in desperate agony, kills himself as well. On hearing the news of her son's death, Eurydice, the queen, also kills herself, cursing Creon.

Alone, in despair, Creon accepts responsibility for all the tragedy and prays for a quick death. The play ends with a somber warning from the chorus that pride will be punished by the blows of fate.

List of Characters

Antigone Daughter of Oedipus. She defies a civil law forbidding the burial of Polynices, her brother, in order to uphold the divine law requiring that the dead be put to rest with proper rituals.

Ismene Sister of Antigone, daughter of Oedipus. She timidly refuses to join her sister in disobeying the civil law, but later wants to join her in death.

Creon King of Thebes, brother-in-law of Oedipus, uncle of Polynices, Antigone, and Ismene. His strict order to leave Polynices' body unburied and his refusal to admit the possibility that he is wrong bring about the events of the tragedy.

Haemon Son of Creon, promised in marriage to Antigone. He argues calmly for Antigone's release, but meets with angry rejection.

A Sentry Who brings news of the attempted burial of Polynices.

Tiresias The blind prophet who advised Laius and Oedipus, before Creon. His auguries show that the gods are angered by Creon's decision to leave Polynices unburied.

Eurydice Queen of Thebes, wife of Creon. On hearing of the death of her son, she kills herself.

A Messenger A man who tells of the deaths of Antigone, Haemon, and Eurydice.

Chorus The elders of Thebes and their Leader. They listen loyally to Creon and rebuke Antigone, but advise the king to change his mind when Tiresias warns of the gods' punishment.

Lines 1-116

Summary

Antigone tells Ismene of her plans to bury their brother Polynices in defiance of Creon's orders. When Ismene refuses to join her sister, pleading their weakness as women and subjects of Creon, Antigone leaves her angrily, determined to bury her brother, even if it means her own death.

Commentary

The opening scene sets up the problem of the play: Creon's strict order to leave Polynices unburied as punishment for his treason, and Antigone's determination to offer her brother the final rituals that will assure his soul's rest.

As an invader of the city and the killer of his brother Eteocles, Polynices represents the enemy of the *polis*, a traitor unworthy of the most basic privileges. For his crimes, and as an example to the city, Creon refuses him burial—the ceremony that will put his soul to rest. The indecency, so abhorrent to Antigone, is meant as a deterrent to anyone who might be tempted to take advantage of this moment of crisis, so soon after the war, to seize power.

And Creon's threat of death to anyone who tries to bury Polynices also stands as a civil defense measure. The death he specifies—stoning—requires the participation of the whole city. Just as the disrespect for Polynices' body is a public display of contempt for traitors, the consequence of stoning unites the city against anyone who feels sympathy for an enemy.

Antigone, Polynices' sister, has a very different view. Outside the city walls—symbolically, outside the law—Antigone looks for Ismene's help in her plan to bury their brother, a duty traditionally carried out by the women of the family. As a sister, Antigone feels she must offer Polynices burial—in fact, she promised him this favor specifically in *Oedipus at Colonus*. With the argument of tradition, and with reminders of their common identity as the children of the doomed Oedipus, Antigone encourages Ismene to join her, literally to lift their brother's body together, to assure him rest.

Character Insight

In this scene, Antigone displays offense at Creon's order. First and foremost, she takes it as a personal rebuke against herself. But she also sees the civil order as forbidding her participation in a rite reserved for women, thus denying her fundamental role in society.

Antigone's anger and determination, though, does not ignite her sister to rebellion. Passive and resigned, Ismene sees her own womanhood as relative weakness. As women and subjects, Ismene demurs, there is nothing they can do.

In rejecting Ismene's passive obedience to the state, Antigone responds to a higher, religious law, a power that overrules even Creon's authority, because leaving the dead unburied—for any reason—offends the gods. To her sister, Antigone makes her declaration that she will obey the gods before the state at whatever cost, even her own life. Antigone will deliver the same passionate, strident speech throughout the drama, unmoved by either pleadings or threats.

In her defiance and her disregard for her own life, Antigone declares her love for the dead, and even, it seems, her love for death itself.

Glossary

Thebes chief city of ancient Boeotia, in eastern central Greece. Here, the location of the tragedy.

Zeus the chief deity of Greek mythology, son of Chronus and Rhea and husband of Hera.

Argos ancient city-state in the northeast Peloponnesus from the seventh century B.C. until the rise of Sparta. Here, used to represent the forces led by Polynices to take back Thebes.

Lines 117-178

Summary

The chorus of elders enters, chanting a song celebrating the recent Theban victory.

Commentary

Literary
Device

The Chorus recreates in imagery the bloody battle to take Thebes. Polynices, the invader at the head of the legendary seven against Thebes, emerges as an eagle—bold, terrifying, and bloodthirsty. Against such a horrendous enemy, the ode implies, any measures are justified, even, perhaps, the most recent order to leave his body unburied.

Thebes itself takes little credit for the victory. Instead, the force from Argos flees the city, according to the chorus, whipped by "the bridle of fate" (124) and blasted by Zeus himself, rather than the efforts of the Theban army. The punishment of the invader, then, must be the direct will of the gods, not of men. Even nature itself seems to herald the victory, as the rising sun represents the return of truth and order to the city. Thebes, blessed by the gods, indulges itself in self-righteous satisfaction, certain of its moral standing.

In the midst of victory, the elders soberly note one exception—the deaths of Eteocles and Polynices, who killed one another, as predicted by their father, Oedipus. Their "common prize of death" (163) leaves the city without a ruler descended from Oedipus. As the chanting ends, the elders look to Creon for a new beginning.

Glossary

Dirce a river of Thebes.

Dionysus the god of wine and revelry.

Lines 179–376

Summary

Creon enters, assuring the elders of Thebes that the city is now safe and pledging to keep it so under his leadership. He formally announces his intention to bury Eteocles with honor and leave Polynices unburied. When Creon hears that someone has performed a simple ritual burial for Polynices, he becomes furious, accuses the sentry of taking bribes, and demands that those responsible be brought to him.

Commentary

In this very political scene, Creon asserts his leadership by right of kinship and by the decisiveness of his first official act—the decision to leave Polynices unburied.

The defilement of Polynices' body represents Creon's calculated decision to punish treason without mercy in order to deter any further uprisings. The physical and spiritual horror of a body unburied, Creon assumes, will remind all citizens of the consequences of challenging the state. Without admitting it publicly, Creon is in fact placing his authority to safeguard the city above the gods' laws concerning respect for the dead. This decision, as well as the tone of his speech about the ideal ruler he hopes to be, makes clear Creon's tendency toward arrogance and pride—characteristics that will become even more apparent as the play progresses.

Sophocles uses dramatic irony to great effect here. The audience knows that Antigone has already decided to defy Creon's orders, and so the new king's rule is already undercut and compromised. Creon will never be the ideal ruler of the stable Thebes he imagines in this scene. Accordingly, the news of Polynices' ritual burial—a merely symbolic sprinkling of dust—unnerves Creon, reducing him to wild accusations and threats. In contrast, in a passage that recalls Antigone's references to religious laws in the first scene, the chorus wonders if the gods themselves had a hand in the ritual. Faced with the first challenge to his leadership, Creon's calm facade cracks, while Antigone, unseen and unnamed, begins to emerge as a heroine.

In response to Creon's stern demand for loyalty, the elders promise obedience, replying "Only a fool could be in love with death" (246). Notice that their response promises obedience, but does not express approval of Creon's plan. Their practical, sensible, and safe perspective contrasts sharply with Antigone's rebellious determination—a passion that seems to embody her own love for death.

Throughout the play, in fact, the men of the chorus seem torn between their loyalty to Creon and their admiration for Antigone. As elders of the city, they must respect both civil and divine law. The drama that unfolds forces them into a difficult choice, which is sometimes reflected in their comments.

Glossary

Laius king of Thebes before his son, Oedipus. Killed by Oedipus before the action of the tragedy Oedipus the King.

Lines 377–416

Summary

The elders chant an ode in praise of man, who is powerful over all things except death.

Commentary

This ode stands as one of the greatest poems written by Sophocles. The breadth of the imagery—celebrating man's power over animals, birds, and even the earth's fertility—gives a feeling of ever-expanding possibility, cut short suddenly by the somber mention of Death.

In the conclusion, the elders propose a pious compromise between man's soaring pride and inevitable mortality. Law and "the justice of the gods" (410) will preserve man and society, the elders intone. The next scene will open the question of how—or even whether—earthly law and heavenly justice can be reconciled with one another.

Lines 417-655

Summary

A sentry brings Antigone to Creon, retelling how he and his men wiped the corpse clean of the dust from the first burial rite and then how they caught Antigone trying to bury Polynices again. Antigone proudly proclaims her guilt to Creon, but also declares that the king had no authority to forbid burial. In disobeying Creon, Antigone claims obedience to a higher law.

The attendants drag Ismene before Creon. When she claims to have helped in the burial, Antigone denies that her sister had any role in the rebellious act. Ismene pleads with Creon to spare her sister's life for the sake of his son Haemon, who is engaged to marry Antigone. Creon refuses and announces his intention to execute Antigone for disobeying his order.

Commentary

Theme

This scene dramatizes the powerful conflict between divine law and civil law that has been building from the opening of the play. When Creon and Antigone face each other, their separate beliefs bring them quickly and passionately to matters of life and death.

Antigone's argument calls for obedience to divine law at all costs. Creon is not Zeus, she declares, and he cannot overturn divine law by civil proclamation. Her thinking is unassailable—of course the dead have burial rights, a basic decency upheld by long tradition.

Character Insight

Inwardly, Creon admits this when he mutters that he must discipline Antigone or risk losing his authority and—he fears—even his manhood. He cannot answer her argument rationally, so he must crush her. "She is the man / If this victory goes to her and she goes free" (541–542), he seethes, and his rage propels him into action that will ultimately doom his whole family.

This scene once again emphasizes Antigone's love for death. Unmoved by Creon's distinction between Eteocles and Polynices—the patriot and the traitor, in his view—Antigone says simply that she chooses to love rather than to hate. Exasperated, Creon mocks Antigone's resolve to face execution with a bitter curse: "love the dead!" (593).

Lines 656–700

Summary

The elders sing an ode affirming the power of the gods over people, from generation to generation, as in the family of Oedipus.

Commentary

Literary Device

The elders mark the moment of Antigone's condemnation with a somber look back to the doom that has followed her family for generations. Like Antigone herself, in the first scene, the chorus points to the power of Zeus as the source of the curse. No one can oppose the will of the gods, the elders chant. Their pious sentiment brings into question Creon's insistence on his own will, and begins to foreshadow a doom that will bring him down as well.

Glossary

Olympus the home of the gods.

Lines 701-878

Summary

Creon's son, Haemon, reasons with his father to change his mind and free Antigone in order to avoid offending those citizens who side with her. Creon rejects his son's advice fiercely and threatens to kill Antigone right in front of him. Haemon leaves, declaring that Creon will never see him again. Alone, Creon tells the chorus that he will let Ismene go, but he intends to wall Antigone up alive, to die of starvation.

Commentary

Haemon's dialogue with his father makes clear Creon's inflexibility and arrogance in this difficult situation. Respectfully, Haemon approaches Creon and offers him information that should have an effect on any rational ruler's decision. The people of Thebes, Haemon reports, have taken Antigone as their heroine and will not tolerate her execution.

Note especially here that Haemon does not plead for Antigone's life on the basis of his love for her or his desire to marry her. Haemon's argument could come from any close advisor, and reason demands that Creon listen and weigh it carefully.

Creon, however, cannot take advice from his son, and the formal conversation breaks down into bickering and accusations. Note that Creon's main charge is that his son has become Antigone's ally—a "woman's accomplice" (837) and "woman's slave" (848)—rather than the supporter of his father, right or wrong. Haemon, like Antigone, appeals to the higher law of the gods, but Creon sees Anarchy—which he personifies as a woman—as the greatest crime of all. Unaware of his own pride and arrogance, Creon thrashes out wildly at all who dare question his authority.

However much he condemns his son, Creon's decision about the method of Antigone's execution indicates that Haemon's argument has had some effect. Conscious that he cannot count on the support of the city—which is essential if Antigone is to be publicly stoned to death— he determines to carry out the sentence in isolation, in a manner that will not involve the people of Thebes at all.

Furthermore, the execution suits Creon because he imagines it will diminish Antigone's strong passion and sense of purpose. In her sealed tomb, Creon gloats, Antigone can worship her only god, Death, and come, too late, to a clear understanding of her wrongs. Ironically, Creon will come to the same understanding about himself, in the conclusion of the drama. For now, however, even Death, in Creon's view, must serve his royal will.

Literary Device

Note that the chorus worries about Haemon's sudden departure, hinting that he may be angry enough to commit some violence. The reference foreshadows the scene in the tomb, when Haemon will attack his father before killing himself.

Lines 879-894

Summary

The chorus of elders chants an ode to the power of love, represented by the mighty goddess Aphrodite.

Commentary

Theme

In this ode, Sophocles introduces the theme of romantic love—a concept new to the Oedipus Trilogy. Reflecting on the conversation between Creon and Haemon, the chorus comes to the conclusion that love is the cause of their conflict.

Haemon has not appealed to his father as a bridegroom for the life of his bride. Instead, Sophocles chooses the chorus—a more objective voice— to remind the audience that not even the gods can resist love's power. The emotional distance of the chorus makes this truth even more convincing, given the situation. If they can see the injustice and argue the case coolly, then Creon's decision must really be wrong.

In taking his son's bride, Creon is offending Aphrodite, the unconquerable goddess, and possibly bringing destruction upon himself and his throne. The chorus' warning represents a rational, objective comment on an emotional, personal situation, making clear that Creon's anger is blinding him to reality.

Glossary

Aphrodite the goddess of love and beauty.

Lines 895–969

Summary

Antigone anticipates her approaching death by singing her own funeral dirge, and the chorus wonders if Oedipus' sins condemned his daughter to her fate.

Commentary

For a woman who has been hailed as a heroine by the city, Antigone suffers a surprising amount of criticism from the chorus. The elders remind her sharply that her death was her own decision, sternly warn her not to compare herself with the gods, and even bring up the shame of her father's tragic ordeal and her incestuous birth.

Although the chorus understands the danger of Creon's arrogance, the elders are not prepared to side with Antigone, or even offer her sympathy. Their tone makes clear that they see her as a willful, passionate girl, caught in a trap of her own making.

The assault breaks through Antigone's mourning as she flares up in anger. "Why can't you wait till I am gone?" (932) she passionately responds, in a return to her characteristic strength. But when the moment fades, the audience sees Antigone sink into a melancholy isolation—the emotional equivalent of the death she will soon face.

Indeed, Antigone expresses her anguish in the very words her father used in *Oedipus the King*: "I am agony!" (967). The curse of Oedipus, it is clear, now has come to rest on his daughter.

Glossary

Acheron a river in Hades, often identified as the river across which Charon ferries the dead.

Niobe a queen of Thebes, daughter of Tantalus, who, weeping for her slain children, is turned into a stone from which tears continue to flow.

Lines 970–1034

Summary

Before Creon orders the guards to take her away to her death, Antigone reflects on her decision to bury her brother and its sad consequences.

Commentary

In the culmination of the continuing theme of loving Death, Antigone calls the chamber where she will be buried alive "my bridal-bed" (978). Faced with the deadly consequences of her action, Antigone seems overwhelmed, even regretful. Only in her last speech does she fully regain her characteristic strength, calling upon the men of Thebes to witness her suffering in the name of divine law.

At Creon's order for the guards to take her away, Antigone nearly crumbles in anguish. Before recovering her courage, she cries out: "Oh, god, the voice of death. It's come, it's here" (1025).

The moment resembles the scene at the conclusion of Verdi's opera *Aida*, when the heroine and her love Ramades—who are also entombed alive—hear their funeral dirge above the sealed chamber, and suddenly despair. In both stories of passionate heroines who embrace death willingly, the drama demands an instant of wild resistance, a proof that the character does in fact cherish the life she is on the verge of losing.

Antigone, the audiences sees, is not a heartless fanatic. She truly mourns the life she leaves, and, at this instant, fears the consequences of her decision.

Also in this scene, rather surprisingly, Antigone explains why she would never have defied Creon's order for the sake of a husband or her own children. The passage seems to contradict Antigone's devotion to the laws of the gods and undercuts her idealism. The tone of her argument seems uncharacteristic of Antigone, who has expressed her convictions strongly all along—even while lamenting her approaching death.

Style & Language

Translator Robert Fagles traces the logic Antigone uses to the *Histories* of Herodotus, in a story of a Persian woman who saves her brother rather than her husband or children. But he adds that Antigone's rationale would make better sense had she been able to save Polynices, rather than just bury him.

The speech, scholars agree, is troubling, and some readers have even raised the possibility that Sophocles did not write it at all. Fagles, however, includes the passage, suggesting that Antigone is speaking to Polynices here, the brother for whom she has sacrificed the possibility of husband and children.

Glossary

Persephone the daughter of Zeus and Demeter, abducted by Hades to be his wife in the lower world. The Queen of Hades.

Lines 1035-1089

Summary

The elders chant an ode about heroes and heroines who endured terrible punishments at the hands of Fate.

Commentary

After finding fault with Antigone for comparing herself to the gods, the elders choose their own legendary figures to compare to Antigone. Danae's cruel imprisonment in a tower mirrors Antigone's fate, and the penetration of Zeus into Danae's chamber looks forward to Haemon's appearance in the tomb. Note that the chorus chooses the mortal Danae to compare with Antigone, rather than the goddess Niobe, as Antigone has done in her lament. As witnesses to the whole sad tale of Oedipus' family, the chorus feels great sympathy for Antigone, but they must stop short of comparing her to the gods. Their responsibility as elders demands that they not glorify someone who is breaking the law.

Literary Device

At the same time, the chorus cannot fully support Creon in his judgment of Antigone. As a warning, then, the chorus switches to another tale, the story of Lycurgus, the king who offended Dionysus by persecuting the god's women worshippers. In championing the laws of the gods, the persecuted women resemble Antigone, and Lycurgus recalls Creon. For his crimes against Dionysus, Lycurgus suffered imprisonment. His punishment foreshadows Creon's fate at the end of the play.

Glossary

Danae the mother of Perseus by Zeus, who visits her in the form of a shower of gold.

Lycurgus real or legendary Spartan lawgiver of about the ninth century B.C. Here, the persecutor of the women who worshipped Dionysus.

Muses the nine goddesses who preside over literature and the arts and sciences: Calliope, Clio, Euterpe, Melpomene, Terpsichore, Erato, Polyhymnia, Urania, and Thalia.

Thrace wild region to the north of Thebes.

Ares the god of war, the son of Zeus and Hera.

Lines 1090-1237

Summary

Tiresias warns Creon that the gods disapprove of the desecration of Polynices' corpse and will punish him with the death of his own son, Haemon. Creon dismisses Tiresias in anger, accusing him, like the sentry, of taking bribes, but declares his determination to bury Polynices and free Antigone.

Commentary

Before Antigone was taken away to die, she cried out: "What law of the mighty gods have I transgressed?" (1013). Faced with death for upholding divine law, Antigone might have expected a miraculous rescue, proof of the gods' protection. Instead, she leaves the city feeling utterly abandoned by the gods.

Theme

In this scene, the blind prophet Tiresias makes clear that the gods are not indifferent to Antigone, although her name is never mentioned. While the gods do not intercede for Antigone directly, Tiresias' ritual augury reveals that her cause—the burial of her brother—is just. The gods, offended by Creon's refusal to bury Polynices, threaten the life of his own son. Given this prophetic warning, the pious response would be to bury Polynices immediately, and—although this is never mentioned—free the woman who upheld the law of the gods. The moral victory, muted as it is, goes to Antigone.

Character Insight

As in *Oedipus the King* and *Oedipus at Colonus*, Tiresias' prophetic truth meets with anger and rejection. Like Oedipus, Creon refuses to believe Tiresias' warning because it contradicts his own sense of responsibility and moral scruples. Like Oedipus, Creon also accuses Tiresias of lying and of using his prophetic power for personal advantage. But unlike Oedipus, Creon proves himself open to persuasion, as he suddenly yields to the prophet's advice and rushes off—too late—to bury Polynices and free Antigone.

Note the paradox of Tiresias' explanation of the gods' fateful justice—a corpse for a corpse—and his summary of Creon's crime: keeping a dead body above ground and placing a living body beneath it. This outrage against the natural order of things springs from Creon's pride and offends the majesty of the gods deeply.

Glossary

augury a divination from omens. Here it refers to the ritual sacrifice of an animal and the examination of its organs for an indication of the future.

Sardis capital of ancient Lydia. Here, a place known for precious metals.

Lines 1238-1273

Summary

The elders rejoice at Creon's decision in a *paean*, or joyful song, to Dionysus.

Commentary

The ecstasy of the chorus imitates the frenzy of Dionysian worship. Exultation wells up at this pivotal moment in the play, as Creon at last yields and seeks to repair the damage his pride has caused.

The paean echoes a similar moment in *Oedipus the King*, when the chorus wonders in awe whether Oedipus is actually the son of a god. As in *Oedipus the King*, the paean will yield in the following episode to tragic revelations, the end of the glorious hope celebrated by the chorus.

Literary Device

Note the mention of Eleusis and the Mysteries—a reference to the secret rites that offered a vision of eternal life to initiates. Sophocles refers to the Eleusian Mysteries throughout *Oedipus at Colonus*, foreshadowing the tragic hero's mystical passing. Here the reference offers hope for Antigone's recovery from her sealed tomb, just as the goddess Persephone escaped from the Underworld.

Glossary

Semele the daughter of Cadmus and the mother of Dionysus.

Mysteries the Eleusian Mysteries, the secret religious rites celebrated at the ancient Greek city of Eleusis in honor of Demeter and Persephone.

Eleusis town in Greece, northwest of Athens; site of an ancient Greek city (also called Eleusis), seat of the Eleusian Mysteries.

Bacchus another name for Dionysus, the god of wine and revelry.

Ismenus a river of Thebes.

Castalia spring on Mount Parnassus, Greece; in ancient times it was sacred to the Muses and was considered a source of poetic inspiration to all who bathed in it.

Nysa a mountain on Euboa, an island that lies off the Attic and Boeotian coastlines.

Lines 1274-1470

Summary

A messenger announces that Antigone has hanged herself and that Haemon, agonized at her death, has also killed himself. On hearing the news, Eurydice, the queen, retreats into the palace where she, too, kills herself after cursing her husband, Creon. Mourning his wife and son, Creon blames himself for all the tragedy that has occurred and prays that his life will end soon.

Commentary

The final scene ends not only *Antigone*, but the entire sequence of tales in the Oedipus Trilogy. After this sad end, with Creon led off in despair, there will be no more possibilities—tragic or otherwise—for the House of Oedipus.

All the tragic events of the episode—Antigone's hanging, Haemon's suicide, the death of the queen—result from Creon's initial determination to ensure the stability of the city by punishing its enemy even after death, and his stubborn insistence on his orders, even when challenged on the grounds of divine law and human decency. Creon's change of heart comes too late to save anyone, but just in time to allow the proud king a last heartbreaking confrontation with his son. In this, fate seems to condemn Creon with particular—perhaps justified—harshness.

Modern readers may wonder why the climactic scene in the tomb is not dramatized on stage. Greek theatrical tradition demanded that scenes of violence be described rather than actually seen. The emphasis of the drama was on poetry and horrifying or shocking action would distract the audience from the power of the words spoken by the actors.

The last scene of *Antigone*, like the final scene of *Oedipus the King*, offers the spectacle of a proud, confident, decisive king brought low by fate. In his first appearance in this play, Creon energetically describes his vision of the ideal king to his people, confident that he will grow into the role with experience. Faced with his failure, Creon suffers not only a loss of self-esteem, but a loss of identity itself, as he cries: "I don't even exist—I'm no one. Nothing" (1446).

Note that in contrast to the philosophical tone of the last lines of *Oedipus the King* and *Oedipus at Colonus*, the chorus in *Antigone* chants a cold, judgmental pronouncement on the tragedy. Rather than offering comfort or wondering in awe at the power of fate, the chorus here implies that Creon gets what he deserves, in a kind of direct divine retribution. The only solace, it seems, is the wisdom the observers can gain in watching the destruction of the proud.

Glossary

Cadmus a Phoenician prince and founder of Thebes; he kills a dragon and sows its teeth, from which many armed men rise, fighting each other, until only five are left to help him build the city.

Hecate a goddess of the moon, earth, and underground realm of the dead, later regarded as the goddess of sorcery and witchcraft.

Pluto the god ruling over the lower world.

Megareus son of Creon and Eurydice. He was killed defending Thebes during the attack of the Seven.

CHARACTER ANALYSES

The following character analyses delve into the physical, emotional, and psychological traits of the literary work's major characters so that you might better understand what motivates these characters. The writer of this study guide provides this scholarship as an educational tool by which you may compare your own interpretations of the characters. Before reading the character analyses that follow, consider first writing your own short essays on the characters as an exercise by which you can test your understanding of the original literary work. Then, compare your essays to those that follow, noting discrepancies between the two. If your essays appear lacking, that might indicate that you need to reread the original literary work or re-familiarize yourself with the major characters.

Oedipus

Born from myth, Sophocles' Oedipus figures as the tragic hero who kills his father and marries his mother. A victim of fate vilified by all, he discovers his own corruption and tears out his eyes in self-punishment—a symbolic castration for his incestuous sin.

The keynote of Oedipus' character lies in his will to know—and, thereby, to control reality. Oedipus' brilliance and determination serve him well in solving mysteries—like the riddle of the Sphinx—but lead ultimately to his tragic downfall.

The petition of the chorus that opens *Oedipus the King* attests to Oedipus' responsible leadership. He has been a good king for Thebes, and in crisis he moves decisively to save his city, but in his excitement and energy, Oedipus lacks discretion. When, for example, Creon hints wisely that they should discuss the news from the oracle in private, Oedipus refuses, insisting that every action he takes to find and to purge corruption from the city must be public.

Impervious to reason and advice, Oedipus follows his will with an intellectual passion. His drive to unearth the mystery—and his pride in performing his intellectual feat before the whole city—end in horror, as he discovers that the object of his relentless search is himself. To the chorus, Oedipus explains his blinding as his mournful inability ever to look upon his loved ones again, but the violence also represents his attack on that part of himself that cannot stop seeking out and finding what is hidden, despite the fateful consequences.

In *Oedipus at Colonus*, the tragic hero persists in his will and determination, despite his age, blindness, and banishment. In contrast to the Oedipus who accepted infamy and begged for punishment at the end of *Oedipus the King*, the Oedipus of *Oedipus at Colonus* maintains furiously that his agonized past was not his fault. All the intellectual passion that he once devoted to solving the mystery of the Sphinx and finding Laius' murderer, he now pours into his self-defense: He did not know that he was doing wrong.

To the end, then, knowledge fires the tragic heart of Oedipus; yet, after his long suffering, he also attains something more profound—wisdom and transcendence. At the end of *Oedipus at Colonus*, Oedipus leads Theseus, king of Athens, and his daughters to his resting place—confidently, as if he has regained his sight—and there, in the place promised to him, he regains his integrity, becoming at one with the power he once sought to escape and to deny.

Creon

Perhaps more than any other figure in the Oedipus Trilogy, Creon, Oedipus' brother-in-law, seems to be a very different character in each of the plays.

In *Oedipus the King*, Creon embodies the voice of reason. As Oedipus storms, Creon maintains his calm; when Oedipus cries out to be banished, Creon protects him with gentle firmness. By the end of the tragedy, Creon proves himself sensible and responsible, a good leader for the now kingless Thebes.

In *Oedipus at Colonus*, in contrast, Creon emerges as wily and manipulative, willing to do anything to gain his ends. When Creon sees that flattering words will not move Oedipus, he has no compunction in holding Antigone and Ismene hostage and threatening Theseus with war. Angry and intent on his will, Creon appears the epitome of the bad, ruthless leader, impervious to the laws of the gods or humanity.

As the king of Thebes in *Antigone*, Creon is a complete autocrat, a leader who identifies the power and dignity of the state entirely with himself. Instead of accepting kingship as a duty—as Creon was prepared to do at the end of *Oedipus the King*—the Creon of *Antigone* maintains the throne as his unquestioned right and rules Thebes by his own will, rather than for the good of the people. Creon's power madness makes him unyielding and vindictive, even to his own son, who speaks as reasonably to him as the Creon of *Oedipus the King* spoke to Oedipus. Full of pride and ambition at the start, by the play's conclusion Creon suffers the wrath of the gods, and ends, in his own words, as "no one. Nothing" (*Antigone* 1446).

Antigone

With the character of Antigone, the reader of the Oedipus Trilogy might get a false impression of watching a young girl grow up, as in a novel or a true series of related plays. Remember that each play of the Oedipus Trilogy stands on its own. Although the stories of the three tragedies are connected, Sophocles did not write them in chronological order, nor did he mean for them to be viewed in a particular sequence.

At the conclusion of *Oedipus the King*, Antigone, with her sister Ismene, represents both the helpless innocence of a child and the undeniable proof of an incestuous union. The audience recognizes her pitiful, two-fold vulnerability, but beyond this she remains silent and unknown.

In *Oedipus at Colonus*, Antigone epitomizes sacrifice and loyalty, caring for her blind, wandering father with no regard for her own needs or aspirations. Antigone's devotion to her father makes her an admirable character on her own, but also raises the audience's opinion of the sometimes cantankerous Oedipus, as a figure able to inspire and keep such love.

As the heroine of *Antigone*, Oedipus' daughter grapples with Fate on her own, not just as a child or a dutiful daughter. Her decisiveness and courage appear in stark contrast to Ismene's passive timidity, and, in this tragedy at least, overshadow even her brother Polynices' bold attempt to take Thebes. In championing the laws of the gods above the laws of the state, Antigone occupies the ultimate high moral ground, but she is not impervious to doubt. Just before she is led off to her death, Antigone mourns the life she is leaving by her own choice and even seems to regret her decision. The moment passes, however, and may represent simply a small proof of human weakness that makes Antigone's strength all the more dramatic.

Ismene

As Oedipus' other daughter—the more prominent being Antigone—Ismene represents primarily a complement and contrast to her sister.

In *Oedipus at Colonus*, Ismene serves her father mostly as an information gatherer, a resident of Thebes who can bring her wandering father and sister news of their home city and the rest of their family. Note that she makes a memorable entrance in the play, riding a colt and wearing a large sun-hat. As Antigone's sister and Oedipus' daughter, Ismene is an especially important character in the drama. Possibly Sophocles chose this unique entrance as a way of marking her as one of the members of the family, rather than just another passerby in Colonus.

Both Ismene and Antigone represent filial duty in *Oedipus at Colonus*, but Ismene takes the less heroic role. Unlike Antigone, Ismene, it seems, has a nearly normal, stable life. She does not serve her father's needs or share his danger daily, as does Antigone. Although Ismene's devotion obviously exceeds her brothers'—even her father praises her to Polynices—it does not equal the sacrifice of Antigone. Ismene is continually in her sister's shadow.

In *Antigone*, Ismene's fear of challenging Creon and the laws of the state prevent her from sharing in her sister's bold plan and, ultimately, her fate. In this play, the closest view of the sisters' relationship, Ismene's words and actions make clear that she loves her sister greatly, but differs from her greatly, too. Unlike Antigone, Ismene seems paralyzed by her cultural identity as a woman. Ismene is emotional rather than passionate, more likely to plead for mercy than demand justice. The last survivor of Oedipus' house after the death of Antigone, Ismene nonetheless seems to vanish at the end, her identity lost in the culmination of the tragedy.

Polynices

In *Oedipus at Colonus*, Polynices represents the son who wishes to reconcile with his father for self-serving reasons. Wily and somewhat shameless, Polynices dares to compare himself with his father, Oedipus, as a fellow outcast—this, despite the fact that Polynices is in part responsible for Oedipus' banishment. The gall of this argument marks Polynices as an opportunist and his ill-fated plan as a simple grab for power.

In contrast to his father, Polynices displays an ability to disregard Fate in favor of his own will. In throwing himself into the plans for the invasion of Thebes despite his father's curse and Antigone's warning, he shows a reckless ambition that compromises both his character and his goal. As the enemy of the villainous Creon, Polynices should emerge as a kind of hero, yet his own arrogance precludes this, and makes him instead a deeply flawed, doomed son and brother of a fate-stricken house.

Theseus

As leader of Athens in *Oedipus at Colonus*, Theseus emerges as the ideal king, the personification of the city-state's vision of itself at its highest point. At the same time of the production of *Oedipus at Colonus*, such a vision of the ideal Athenian was comforting to the war-torn Athenian audience. Theseus possesses, it seems, every Athenian virtue. He is diplomatic in negotiating with the prickly Oedipus, pious in his concern for the sacred precinct and the will of the gods, strong in opposing the bullying Creon, courteous in his introduction of Polynices, and decisive in driving off the Theban intruders. A contrast to the violent Creon and the reckless Polynices, as well as a benefactor to Oedipus himself, Theseus handles a difficult situation with political skill. In this, he represents one of the very few unflawed characters in the Oedipus Trilogy.

Tiresias

The blind prophet of Thebes appears in *Oedipus the King* and *Antigone*. In both plays, he represents the same force—the truth rejected by a willful and proud king, almost the personification of Fate itself.

Tiresias comes to Oedipus against his will, not wanting to explain the meaning of the oracle to the king, but he goes freely to Creon in *Antigone*, with news of his own augury. In both cases, however, after a courteous greeting, Tiresias meets with insults and rejection. Never surprised by abuse, Tiresias does not back down when threatened. True to the gift of prophetic power, he stands unflinching before the fury of kings. His speech may be barbed, his message horrifying, but Tiresias' dedication to the truth is uncompromising. For his suffering, his piety, and his devotion to prophetic truth, Tiresias emerges as a powerful—even admirable—character in the Oedipus Trilogy.

Jocasta

At once Oedipus' mother and his wife, Jocasta represents the most immediate victim of Oedipus' fate, after the tragic hero himself. In contrast to Oedipus, Jocasta distrusts the oracles and believes that whatever happens will happen by unforeseeable chance. Still, she is wary enough to honor Apollo with offerings in a crisis.

Intelligent and capable, but not driven to exploration as Oedipus is, Jocasta has her own philosophy about what should be known or looked into. When Jocasta realizes before Oedipus the reality of his identity, she begs him to stop his questioning to avoid grief. Later, her own panicked grief impels her to suicide.

Eurydice

Creon's wife appears briefly in *Antigone*, when she hears of her son Haemon's death. Pious and discreet, she retreats to the palace, evidently to mourn in privacy, as her nature would dictate. The news that she has cursed Creon and stabbed herself to death shocks the chorus—and the audience—since such violence and anger seem out of character. In this, Eurydice proves the power of Fate to destroy personality itself, and transform a gentle, quiet woman into a figure of fury and despair.

CRITICAL ESSAYS

On the pages that follow, the writer of this study guide provides critical scholarship on various aspects of Sophocles' *Oedipus Trilogy*. These interpretive essays are intended solely to enhance your understanding of the original literary work; they are supplemental materials and are not to replace your reading of the *Oedipus Trilogy*. When you're finished reading the *Oedipus Trilogy*, and prior to your reading this study guide's critical essays, consider making a bulleted list of what you think are the most important themes and symbols. Write a short paragraph under each bullet explaining why you think that theme or symbol is important; include at least one short quote from the original literary work that supports your contention. Then, test your list and reasons against those found in the following essays. Do you include themes and symbols that the study guide author doesn't? If so, this self test might indicate that you are well on your way to understanding original literary work. But if not, perhaps you will need to reread the *Oedipus Trilogy*.

The Power of Fate in the Oedipus Trilogy

Are people truly responsible for their actions? This question has puzzled humanity throughout history. Over the centuries, people have pondered the influence of divine or diabolical power, environment, genetics, even entertainment, as determining how free any individual is in making moral choices.

The ancient Greeks acknowledged the role of Fate as a reality outside the individual that shaped and determined human life. In modern times, the concept of Fate has developed the misty halo of romantic destiny, but for the ancient Greeks, Fate represented a terrifying, unstoppable force.

Fate was the will of the gods—an unopposable reality ritually revealed by the oracle at Delphi, who spoke for Apollo himself in mysterious pronouncements. The promise of prophecy drew many, but these messages usually offered the questioner incomplete, maddenly evasive answers that both illuminated and darkened life's path. One famous revelation at Delphi offered a general the tantalizing prophesy that a great victory would be won if he advanced on his enemy. The oracle, however, did not specify to whom the victory would go.

By the fifth century, B.C., Athenians frankly questioned the power of the oracle to convey the will of the gods. Philosophers such as Socrates opened rational debate on the nature of moral choices and the role of the gods in human affairs. Slowly, the belief in a human being's ability to reason and to choose gained greater acceptance in a culture long devoted to the rituals of augury and prophecy. Socrates helped to create the Golden Age with his philosophical questioning, but Athens still insisted on the proprieties of tradition surrounding the gods and Fate, and the city condemned the philosopher to death for impiety.

Judging from his plays, Sophocles took a conservative view on augury and prophecy; the oracles in the Oedipus Trilogy speak truly— although obliquely—as an unassailable authority. Indeed, this voice of the gods—the expression of their divine will—represents a powerful, unseen force throughout the Oedipus Trilogy.

Yet this power of Fate raises a question about the drama itself. If everything is determined beforehand, and no human effort can change the course of life, then what point is there in watching—or writing— a tragedy?

According to Aristotle, theater offers its audience the experience of pity and terror produced by the story of the hero brought low by a power greater than himself. In consequence, this catharsis—a purging of high emotion—brings the spectator closer to a sympathetic understanding of life in all its complexity. As the chorus at the conclusion of *Antigone* attests, the blows of Fate can gain us wisdom.

In Greek tragedy, the concept of character—the portrayal of those assailed by the blows of Fate—differs specifically from modern expectations. Audiences today expect character exploration and development as an essential part of a play or a film. But Aristotle declared that there could be tragedy *without* character—although not without action.

The masks worn by actors in Greek drama give evidence of this distinction. In *Oedipus the King*, the actor playing Oedipus wore a mask showing him simply as a king, while in *Oedipus at Colonus*, Oedipus appears in the mask of an old man. As Sophocles saw him—and as actors portrayed him—Oedipus displayed no personality or individuality beyond his role in the legend. The point of the drama, then, was not to uncover Oedipus' personal motivations but to describe the arc of his fall, so as to witness the power of Fate.

In his plays, Shakespeare also created tragedy that revolved around a heroic character who falls from greatness. But Shakespeare's heroes appear fully characterized and their tragedies develop as much from their own conscious intentions as from Fate. Macbeth, for example, pursues his goal of the throne ruthlessly, with murderous ambition. When the witches' prophecies, upon which he has based his hopes, turn out to be just as misleading as any oracle's pronouncement at Delphi, the audience is more likely to blame Macbeth for his heartless ambition than to bemoan his fate with him.

In contrast, Sophocles' hero—even with his tragic flaw (as Aristotle terms it)—maintains the audience's sympathy throughout the drama. The flaw of his character represents less a vicious fault and more a vulnerability, or a blind spot. Oedipus' brilliance, then, is matched by his overconfidence and rashness—a habit of mind that makes him prey to the very fate he wishes to avoid.

Significantly, Oedipus' desperate attempt to escape Fate arises not from ambition or pride, but from an understandable and pious desire to live without committing heinous offenses. Prudently, he decides never to return to the kingdom where the people he believes to be his parents rule. But when an overbearing man on the road nearly runs him down and then cuffs him savagely, Oedipus rashly kills his attacker, who turns out be his father. So, just as he thinks himself free of his fate, Oedipus runs right into it—literally, at a crossroads.

In *Oedipus the King*, Oedipus displays his characteristic brilliance and overconfidence in what he regards as his heroic search for the murderer of Laius. He pursues the mystery relentlessly, confident that its solution will yield him the same glory he enjoyed when he answered the riddle of the Sphinx. Oedipus' self-assurance that he has taken care of his fate blinds him to it and begins the fall that will end in his literal blindness. Thus he becomes the victim—rather than the conquerer—of Fate.

In *Antigone*, Creon also displays a blind spot. Wrapped up in the trappings of power, Creon puts his responsibility for Thebes above the laws of the gods and has to be reminded of the gods' will by Tiresias. Creon's last-minute attempt to conform to the gods' wishes only reveals to him his own inescapable fate—the destruction of his family and the end of his rule.

Antigone herself is painfully aware of the power of Fate, attributing all the tragedy in her family to the will of Zeus. When she acts decisively, choosing to obey the laws of the gods rather than the laws of the state, she seems almost like a modern heroine—a model of individual courage and responsibility. Yet, before her death, Antigone shrinks in horror, acknowledging that she has acted only within the rigid constraints of Fate; indeed, in that moment, her earnestness and conviction fade as she feels the approach of her own doom. Antigone, like the rest of her family, must yield to Fate—the curse that hangs over the house of Oedipus.

Oedipus at Colonus features prolonged debate and protestations over Fate, before granting a unique blessing to the suffering hero. By the time of the story, a sullen Oedipus has grown used to his role as the pariah, the greatest sinner in the world. Still, he argues to the chorus that he did not consciously or willfully commit any crimes. At this point—the end of his life—Oedipus concedes the power of Fate as the reason for his destruction; at the same time, he embraces Fate in his death and fights vigorously to meet his end as the gods promised—at peace and as a benefit to the city where he is buried. Ironically, then, the victim of Fate becomes part of the force that has tortured him; his will to reward and to punish becomes as powerful as the will of the gods themselves.

In *Oedipus at Colonus*—Sophocles' last play—the dramatist seems intent on making a peace between the power of Fate and his willful, all too human hero. The chants of the chorus, as well as the formal, poetic speeches of the characters, suggest that Oedipus' heroic suffering results in a profound transformation into godlike glory. As tragic and terrible as the story of the Oedipus Trilogy is, then, Sophocles grants his audience the hope that the blows of Fate lead not only to wisdom, but to transcendence.

Ritual and Transcendence in the Oedipus Trilogy

In the great amphitheater of Athens, curious tourists can see an inscription on each of the marble seats of honor near the stage: *Reserved for the priest of Dionysus*. The carved letters, still readable after 2,500 years, attest to the religious significance of the theater in the culture of ancient Greece.

For the Greeks of the fifth century B.C., the theater represented a sacramental place, where the actors and audience joined together to worship. The drama—whatever its subject—was an offering to the gods, a ritual that might bring blessing to the city.

The stage itself, actually a dancing area in the style of a threshing floor, recalled the most ancient forms of communal worship. At harvest, people traditionally celebrated the culmination of the growing season by worshipping the god of vegetation in wild, frenzied dances. At the Festival of Dionysus, the stage became a more sophisticated platform for a similar experience—the masked actors' loss of self in music and art for the creation of an emotional closeness with divine power. And the chorus, while chanting their poetry, maintained the simplicity of the older tradition in their obligatory dancing.

Sophocles underscores the connections between drama and the traditions of the fertility god in *Oedipus the King*. Evidence of the trouble in Thebes emerges as a plague, a blight on the land that ruins crops and causes women to miscarry. The close association of human and vegetative fertility—and the connection of both to the capability of the king—represents one of the earliest forms of religious belief. In Sophocles' time, the mysterious but vital union of humans and nature still informed the culture. Accordingly, Oedipus' immorality—however unconscious—pollutes the land, and only his removal and punishment will bring back life to Thebes. In this context, Sophocles offers a ritual of death and rebirth, as well as a formal tragedy in *Oedipus the King*.

In *Oedipus at Colonus* and *Antigone*, Sophocles refers to a particular ritual that inspired and uplifted many of his contemporaries, the Eleusian Mysteries, a rite that offered its initiates the assurance of eternal life. In *Antigone*, when Creon decides to honor the gods' laws by burying Polynices and freeing Antigone, the chorus rejoices with a triumphal paean (joyful song) to Dionysus, calling him "King of the Mysteries!" (1243). The evocation of the god and the mention of the rites at Eleusis underscore Antigone's premature burial and the expected joy of her return to life, the promise offered to the initiates of the Mysteries themselves.

The references to the Mysteries in *Oedipus at Colonus* that extend throughout the drama in the chanted odes of the chorus prepare for the conclusion of the play and the end of Oedipus' life. The poetic allusions to the narcissus, the sacred flower associated with the Mysteries, and the mention of the "awesome rites" (1199) of Eleusis keep before the audience the hope of life after death. At the end of the tragedy, when Theseus witnesses the passing of Oedipus, a messenger delivers a description of the hero's last moments that seems more a mystical transcendence than the death of an old man. The promise of Eleusis, the audience can infer, has been made real in the passing of Oedipus into eternal life.

Of the Eleusian Mysteries itself, modern readers know very little since those who celebrated were sworn to secrecy. But the ritual represented a powerful, transforming experience for many, including the great Roman orator and philosopher, Marcus Tullius Cicero (104–43 B.C.), who praised the Eleusian Mysteries as the source of civilization itself.

The Mysteries recreated in imagination the search of the goddess Demeter for her daughter Persephone (also called Kore), and so demanded a form of personal identification with a divine figure, culminating in an intense religious (and dramatic) experience. The rite began with a procession from Athens to Eleusis, where initiates fasted, sacrificed offerings, and drank a special potion made from barley. At some later time, the initiates were blindfolded and led in darkness to an underground cave where—in some unknown manner—they experienced a kind of death, terrifying beyond words.

Afterwards, standing together in the darkness of an underground chamber, the initiates saw a vision of Kore herself, rising glorious from the depths of the underworld. As fires illuminated the chamber, the ritual celebrant held up a single stalk of wheat, proof of the gods' blessings and the regeneration of life. The initiates rejoiced ecstatically, purged of fear, and confident, as they attested, that eternal life was theirs.

Sophocles himself, in a fragment from *Triptolemus*, wrote of the blessings of life after death granted to those who had experienced the transforming dread and glory of the Eleusian Mysteries. And in his plays, as Aristotle explains, Sophocles proved to be a master in evoking the pity and terror and producing the emotional catharsis that defines tragedy. Like the Eleusian Mysteries, Sophocles' tragedies create a powerful emotional—even religious—experience: The terror of a heroic self crumbling under the blows of Fate, followed by the purging of fear and the coming of wisdom.

Sophocles' continued references to the Eleusian Mysteries indicate his high regard for their power. It may be that in his drama, Sophocles was striving to capture a comparable intense experience of dread relieved by hope and wisdom in an open, public context. For the original audience and centuries of readers, the experience of the tragedies of the Oedipus Trilogy, like a mystical ritual, gives a new birth to the human spirit and, perhaps, makes possible civilization itself.

CliffsNotes Review

Use this CliffsNotes Review to test your understanding of the original text, and reinforce what you've learned in this book. After you work through the identify the quote section, review and essay questions, and the fun and useful practice projects, you're well on your way to understanding a comprehensive and meaningful interpretation of Sophocles' *Oedipus Trilogy*.

Identify the Quote

1. "Blind who now has eyes, beggar who now is rich, he will grope his way toward a foreign soil, a stick tapping before him step by step."

2. "What should a man fear? It's all chance, chance rules our lives. Not a man on earth can see a day ahead, groping through the dark. Better to live at random, best we can."

3. "Die! Die by your own blood brother's hand—die!—Killing the very man who drove you out!"

4. "Show me a man who longs to live a day beyond his time who turns his back on a decent length of life, I'll show the world a man who clings to folly."

5. "Like father, like daughter, passionate, wild . . . she hasn't learned to bend before adversity"

6. "Take me away, quickly, out of sight. I don't even exist—I'm no one. Nothing."

Answers: (1) [(*Oedipus the King*, 517-519) Tiresias' prophecy of Oedipus' fate once he learns his true identity.] (2) [(*Oedipus the King*, 1069-1072) Jocasta, advising Oedipus not to worry about oracles and prophecies.] (3) [(*Oedipus at Colonus*, 1572-1574) Oedipus, cursing Polynices and Eteocles for their part in his banishment. The quotation looks forward to the invasion of Thebes and the events of *Antigone*.] (4) [(*Oedipus at Colonus*, 1378-1380) Inspired by Oedipus' suffering, the chorus sings an ode on the pains of old age.] (5) [(*Antigone*, 525-527) The Leader of the chorus comments to Creon on Antigone's independent spirit.] (6) [(*Antigone*, 1445-1446) Creon expresses his guilt and despair upon the deaths of his wife and son.]

Essay Questions

1. Near the end of each play in the Oedipus Trilogy, a messenger describes what has happened offstage, usually the most important action in the play. Why do you think Sophocles handles the action in this way? How does the off-stage action—left to the imagination—function in the play?

2. Choose one tragedy and discuss the role of the chorus. Does the chorus change over the course of the play? How does the chorus affect the action? How does it focus and intensify the audience's responses?

3. In *Antigone*, who is the real main character—Antigone or Creon? Make a case to support your choice.

4. In *Oedipus the King*, Jocasta, like Oedipus, sees the horror of her identity unfolding. Compare Jocasta to the tragic hero. What are her own ideas about Fate and prophecy? How does she react to her suspicions about Oedipus' birth? How does her final despair differ from Oedipus'?

5. Discuss the differences between Antigone and Ismene in their views of women in society. How does each sister's view shape the choices she makes in the play? How consistent is each in her view?

6. Choose a character who appears in two or more plays of the Oedipus Trilogy, and discuss the similarities and differences in characterization in the plays.

7. Write an essay in which you agree or disagree with the following statement: *Antigone* is primarily a drama of politics, not of fate.

8. As a prophet, Tiresias speaks for the gods and for Fate. How does the character of Tiresias function dramatically in *Oedipus the King* and *Antigone*?

Practice Projects

Plan and write your own scene dramatizing an event not staged in the Oedipus Trilogy. You might choose to dramatize the life of Ismene after the events of *Antigone*, or the encounter of Oedipus with the Sphinx.

Choose a scene from one of the plays of the Oedipus Trilogy and produce it for the class. Design costumes and masks in the style of fifth-century Athens, or have actors wear street clothes.

Design a Web page on the Oedipus Trilogy, featuring themes, legends, or interpretations the class finds particularly helpful or interesting. Correspond by e-mail or post with other classes studying the Oedipus Trilogy.

Using library reference materials, research the Eleusian Mysteries. Present your findings about this tradition to the class in an oral presentation featuring illustrations of the legend of Demeter and Persephone.

Play a recording of the last scene of Verdi's opera *Aida*, beginning with Ramades' "La fatal pietra." Discuss the similarities of this scene with the description of Antigone and Haemon's meeting in the tomb. How does opera compare to classical tragedy? Choose a scene from one of the plays of the Oedipus Trilogy and set it to music for presentation as an operatic drama.

CliffsNotes Resource Center

The learning doesn't need to stop here. CliffsNotes Resource Center shows you the best of the best—links to the best information in print and online about the playwright and/or related works. And don't think that this is all we've prepared for you; we've put all kinds of pertinent information at www.cliffsnotes.com. Look for all the terrific resources at your favorite bookstore or local library and on the Internet. When you're online, make your first stop www.cliffsnotes.com where you'll find more incredibly useful information about Sophocles' *Oedipus Triology*.

Books

This CliffsNotes book provides a meaningful interpretation of Sophocles' *Oedipus Trilogy* published by Houghton Mifflin Harcourt. If you are looking for information about the playwright and/or related works, check out these other publications:

The Sophoclean Chorus: A Study of Character and Function, by Cynthia P. Gardiner. This work pays special attention to the role of the chorus in the Oedipus Trilogy and Sophocles' other tragedies. A concluding essay, "The Choral Character," synthesizes Gardiner's views into an interesting reading of classical drama. Iowa City: Iowa University Press, 1987.

Sophocles, by Ruth Scodel. Part of the Twayne's World Author Series, this study closely examines the life and work of Sophocles. It includes separate chapters on the three plays of the Oedipus Trilogy, and also offers a helpful chronology. Boston: G.K. Hall and Company, 1984.

Vision and Stagecraft in Sophocles, by David Seale. The study includes a detailed account of the actual production of Greek drama, so far as modern classicists and historians have been able to know it. Chapters on each of the plays of the Oedipus Trilogy discuss how the poetry of the tragedies blends with the appearance of the masked actors to create powerful drama. Chicago: University of Chicago Press, 1982.

Sophocles' Tragic World: Divinity, Nature, Society, by Charles Segal. Examines Sophocles' own view of the connections between family, city, nature, and the supernatural. Chapters devoted to individual works, including the plays of the Oedipus Trilogy, detail the effects of a particular tragic world view on the drama. Cambridge, Massachusetts: Harvard University Press, 1995.

The Greek Way to Western Civilization, by Edith Hamilton. A highly acclaimed writer on classical myths provides a very readable introduction to Sophocles. Of particular note is her comparison of Sophocles with the earlier playwright, Aeschylus. New York: W.W. Norton, 1958.

A Study of Sophoclean Drama, G. M. Kirkwood. This work is an enduring study of Sophoclean drama. Kirkwood discusses, for example, Sophocles' highly inventive use of the chorus in his drama. Ithaca, NY: Cornell University Press, 1958.

Greek Tragedy: A Literary Study. 3rd. edition. H.D.F. Kitto has written extensively on Greek culture, and here provides insights on Greek tragedy. This work includes a study of Sophocles' innovations—particularly the introduction of the third actor. London: Metheun, 1966.

Twentieth-Century Interpretations of Oedipus Rex, Michael O'Brien, ed. This collection offers a selection of modern critical views on the tragedy Oedipus the King. The second half of the book includes "View Points" ranging from Plutarch to Marshall McLuhan. A very useful chronology juxtaposes Sophocles' life with the events of his age. Englewood Cliffs, NJ: Prentice-Hall, 1968.

Sophocles: A Collection of Critical Essays, Thomas Woodard, ed. This volume provides a selection of critical interpretations of Sophocles as part of the series "Twentieth-Century Views." Topics include the nature of Sophoclean tragedy and readings of the plays of the Oedipus Trilogy. It also includes views by Friedrich Nietzsche, Sigmund Freud, and Virginia Woolf. Englewood Cliffs, NJ: Prentice-Hall, 1966.

It's easy to find books published by Houghton Mifflin Harcourt. You can find them in your favorite bookstores (on the Internet and at a store near you). We also have two Web sites that you can use to read about all the books we publish:

■ www.cliffsnotes.com

■ www.dummies.com

Internet

Check out these Web resources for more information about *Sophocles' Oedipus Trilogy*:

Ancient Greek Theatre, http://users.groovy.gr/~ekar/ index.html —is a site offering visual and textual background on fifth-century drama in Athens. It includes historical maps of ancient Greece, photographs of theatrical masks used in performance of classical tragedy, and a description and schematic map of an actual fifth-century Greek theater.

Literature On-Line, http://vccslitonline.cc.va.us/oedipus thewreck—this college site includes extensive background on the plays of the Oedipus Trilogy. Visitors may join in a readers' forum, or choose to explore other related Oedipus sites via the links provided.

Hanover College, http://history.hanover.edu/ancient/ sophocle.htm—offers several translations of Sophocles' plays for downloading.

Next time you're on the Internet, don't forget to drop by www.cliffs notes.com. We created an online Resource Center that you can use today, tomorrow, and beyond.

Films

Oedipus the King (1967). Directed by Victor Saville, this film stars Christopher Plummer as Oedipus and features Orson Welles in a powerful performance as Tiresias. It was filmed at the ancient Greek theatre at Dodona.

Send Us Your Favorite Tips

In your quest for knowledge, have you ever experienced that sublime moment when you figure out a trick that saves time or trouble? Perhaps you realized you were taking ten steps to accomplish something that could have taken two. Or you found a little-known workaround that achieved great results. If you've discovered a useful tip that helped you understand

Sophocles or the Oedipus Trilogy more effectively and you'd like to share it, the CliffsNotes staff would love to hear from you. Go to our Web site at www.cliffsnotes.com and click the Talk to Us button. If we select your tip, we may publish it as part of CliffsNotes Daily, our exciting, free e-mail newsletter. To find out more or to subscribe to a newsletter, go to www.cliffsnotes.com on the Web.

Index

CliffsNotes

LITERATURE NOTES

Check Out the All-New CliffsNotes Guides